D1725485

127

HOME-BASED
JOB & BUSINESS
IDEAS

* Best Places to Find Jobs to Work from Home
* TOP Home-Based Business Opportunities
* From Basic Experience to Expert Level
* Grouped by Interests & Hobbies

by Gundi Gabrielle

Copyright © 2019 by Happy Dolphin Enterprises LLC

All rights reserved. No part of this book may be reproduced or transmitted in any form or by any means, electronic, or mechanical, including photocopying, recording, or by any information storage and retrieval system, without written permission from the author, except by a reviewer who may quote brief passages in a review.
SassyZenGirl.com

The following trademarks are owned by *Happy Dolphin Enterprises, LLC:* SassyZenGirl®, Influencer Fast Track®, The Sassy Way®, When You Have No Clue®, Dream Clients On Autopilot®, #ClaimYourFREEDOM®, #ShareYourAWESOME™

First Edition Paperback: August 2019

ISBN: 9781688787568

The Cataloging-In-Publication Data is on file with the Library of Congress.

While all attempts have been made to verify the information provided in this publication, neither the author, nor the publisher assumes any responsibility for errors, omissions, or contrary interpretations on the subject matter herein. This book is for informational purposes only. The views expressed are those of the author alone, and should not be taken as expert instructions or commands. No guarantees for earnings or any other results - of any kind - are being made by the author or publisher, nor are any liabilities being assumed. The reader is entirely responsible for his or her own actions.

Resources marked with an (*) are affiliate products, meaning the author receives a referral fee on any purchase at no extra expense to the purchaser. All products recommended have been tested by the author. Reader or purchaser are advised to do their own research before making any purchase online. No guarantees of earnings or other results - of any kind - nor any liability is assumed for the publisher or author. The reader is entirely responsible for his or her own actions.

Adherence to all applicable laws and regulations, including international, federal, state, and local governing professional licensing, business practices, advertising, and all other aspects of doing business in the US, Canada, or any other jurisdiction is the sole responsibility of the reader or purchaser. Neither the author nor the publisher assumes any responsibility or liability whatsoever on the behalf of the purchaser or reader of these materials. Any perceived slight of any individual or organization is purely unintentional.

This is a **SassyZenGirl** *Guide*

FREE Home Biz Starter Gift:

To help you get started with a bang, stop wasting time and avoid beginner mistakes, I created this

FREE Cheatsheet:

You can Download it HERE:

SassyZenGirl.com/Rookie-Mistakes

TABLE OF CONTENTS

This book features hundreds of resources for companies that hire, places where you can promote your business - and much more.

Rather than having to re-type all urls, you can access a **PDF-Version *with direct, clickable links at***:

HomeBasedBiz.net

In this print version you will only usually find the name of the resource in bold. Just refer to the PDF for the direct link.

Read this first

Welcome... :)

Great to have you & I'm excited to share a vast array of home-based job and business options with you - all the way from "quick cash now" to full fledged business and even franchise opportunities.

In the course of writing over 10 books on business and marketing, I frequently heard from readers how they were struggling to afford necessary software or training when they were first starting out, so I wanted to remedy that situation once and for all by providing a massive list of home-based options for varying needs.

Whether you **need quick cash now** to make ends meet and move on to the next level...

Or you are **doing well financially, but would love to work from home**, rather than missing your kids and stress out in a corporate job...

You will find plenty of options here.

Some with no or very little investment all the way to full franchise options.

Most can be done from the comfort of your home - choosing your own hours.

A few will engage you in your local area, but you still choose your own hours - *part- or full-time* - and can scale as you wish.

NEED CASH NOW?

If you urgently need money right now, I suggest signing up to most options (and platforms) that apply to you in *Basic & Intermediate Skills* as well as *Local Gigs*, so you always have enough options.

Some well-paid gigs limit the amount of assignments you can do per week or month.

No problemo!
Simply sign up to all available platforms and you should always have a steady supply of gigs coming in.

A DEDICATED EMAIL ADDRESS

I suggest creating a dedicated email address just for gig notifications, so you don't miss any.

Don't use hotmail, web.de, or similar low storage providers as your allowed storage will fill up quickly and you will miss important emails without ever knowing it.

Gmail is a good solution and looks more professional, plus, offers additional business tools in the G Suite should you need them down the road.

Also... *(and this should be obvious... :)*

Always check your spam folder - daily!

If you do, it will only take a minute per day, but you will notice how often you would have missed important mails. Happens to me at least a few times a week.

ONLINE vs. LOCAL

The boundaries of what constitutes "home-based" are not always cut'n dry. In this book, it will mean:

Any job or business that allows you to work with your own schedule - when you want and how much you want.

Whether that happens exclusively online in the comfort of your home (= the majority of options in this book) or in your local area, doesn't matter all that much for the purposes of this book. The point is to help you get access to available jobs right now - without having to commit to fixed hours or a minimum time requirement.

Allowing you to add these jobs to whatever you are currently doing while transitioning out of the rat race 9-5 into a long term business or freelance solution that you enjoy and that pays you well.

Cool?

HOME-BASED BUSINESS IDEAS

Similarly, the boundaries between "job" and "business" are often fluid. Freelancer gigs are a typical example.
If you build a large, committed client base, you are certainly running a "business" - even if it may have started with a few freelance "gigs".

Good training will be crucial no matter what you pursue. You are learning a new profession and you don't want to waste time on beginner mistakes and reinventing the wheel when this could have easily been avoided.

It is much easier - and more time efficient - to follow strategies and methods that have already proven to work and I'm including further training options in most chapters to get you up and running quickly.

VIGNETTE STYLE

Obviously with such a long list, each idea is described in a short vignette to give you an overview and something to consider. Where necessary, additional information or training resources are provided, so you can explore further where your interest takes you, as well as an abundance of links to companies that hire and platforms to promote your business.

INTERNATIONAL READERS

Some job and business options are US based only, however, you will often find the same job or business "type" in your country if you just Google it. Once you know the option exists, it will be much easier to find similar offers in your region and language.

PASSIVE INCOME LONG TERM

This book mostly focuses on non passive business options, often starting on a freelance basis. For Passive Income I wrote a separate book in the same series at: **PassiveIncomeFreedom.com**

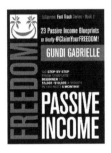

In some cases, there is overlap, and in quite a few cases, you can eventually transition to a mostly passive income model by building a team of freelancers or VAs ("Virtual Assistants") to run the day to day, while you mostly focus on growing your company - or traveling the world.... :)

Long term, you definitely want a few passive income streams, even if you greatly enjoy what you do.

There is a big difference between *having* to work and *choosing* to work.

Initially, if you just need money right now, or you want to get out of *that* job and away from *that* boss, passive or "active" won't matter much, but always keep it in the back of your mind for long term planning.

EXPERIENCE LEVEL

The first half of this book covers a general array of home-based jobs grouped by experience level, from simple jobs - both online and local - to intermediate, pro level and college degree required.

The Basic Level chapter includes a lot of so-called microtask gigs. Small tasks that often only take 10-20 minutes to complete and that people frequently do in their lunch break or while waiting for something.

YOUR HOME & CAR

You will also find a chapter each on how to monetize your home and car - and no, not just AirBnB and

Uber! There is a lot more you can do and some of it quite well paid - *and fun!*

YOUR PASSIONS & HOBBIES

The second half of this book focuses on jobs and business ideas within special interests and hobbies. You will find some really fun ones here that you probably never heard of before...

UPDATES

While all links and resources *(hundreds of them)* have been checked at the time of publishing and will be re-checked from time to time, it is impossible to keep track of every single resource *all* the time .

Therefore, if you find a link not working or a resource no longer available, please let us know at **contact@sassyzengirl.com** and we'll update right away.

Same with additional resources you feel would be helpful to other readers. We'll be happy to credit you if we add them to the book.

SUPPORT

Throughout your journey, feel free to join us in the *SassyZenGirl Networking Group* for support and encouragement. Also, for reviews, feedback, partnerships and other help you might need. It's called the *"friendliest business group on Facebook"* for a reason...:) and everything becomes a lot easier when you don't have to go it alone.

Join us at: **SassyZenGirl.Group**

A FUN ADVENTURE... :)

Now I invite you on a fun journey through a vast array of home-based job and business ideas, including a number of options that will allow you to turn your passions and hobbies into a viable business. Where "work" feels more like fun and you can't wait to get up in the morning to get started. - *Sound exciting?*

Then let's get started!

PART 1
General Job & Business Ideas

Basic Skills

Social Media Moderator

Social Media Moderators monitor clients' social media accounts, in particular, comments and content, weeding out spammers and trolls, answering questions and admitting new group members where applicable.

If you have basic social media and good people skills, this is an easy gig and usually comes with flexible hours. Available wherever you are in the world.

Beyond social media, moderators are also needed to monitor comments and questions on blogs, forums and chat rooms.

These services hire remote moderators:

The Social Element
Women owned and run. Hiring community & engagement managers around the world - *multilingual*.

Crisp Thinking
UK and US based. Community/Social Media moderation and crisis management.

ICUC
Both English and French. Community & social media moderation.

99DollarSocial
Social Media moderation

LiveWorld
Social Media and community moderation.

ModSquad
Forums, social media groups, customer chats

Zynga
Occasionally has openings for "Player Support Managers" for their large collection of online games.

Paid Forum Posting
More for content writers, but also monitoring forum comments in the process.

"Mock" Juror

Yes, you can participate in mock trials as a juror and get paid per "verdict"!

Pay is decent and work can be quite interesting though is usually sporadic. A nice side gig, not replacing a regular full time income.

You must be a US citizen (or any country that works with a jury system), not affiliated with any law firm and not have prior felony convictions. In addition, you need to live in the same judicial district as the trial, which might limit your options.

Mock trials are used by attorneys:

• as a practice run
• to help them decide whether to take a case
• how to approach a case

Having a mock jury helps attorneys to get a feel of how a typical jury would respond, how their arguments come across and how a juror would look at a case.

There are two options:

1) In-person - usually for a full day

More time intensive, but also paying a lot more - up to $150 per day (often incl. lunch).

You will participate in a mock trial in a hotel conference room or similar, and then share your thoughts and impressions in a discussion together with your verdict.

You can check your local newspaper or apply to these companies:

Sign up Direct

National Legal Research

Advanced Jury Research

2) Virtual/Online Juror

As an online juror, you will either watch or read about the case facts and then render your verdict. Usually takes 15-60 minutes per case from the comfort of your home. Virtual juries usually work as a pool of 50+ jurors per case.

Here are several companies that you can sign up to. Fees might change and also depend on length and complexity of each case. Numbers are quoted from the companies' websites:

Online Verdict - $20-60 (cases take about 20-60)
JuryTest - $5-50 per case
eJury - $5-10 per case
Resolution Research
offers a number of different focus groups (consumer, B2B, Medical - and also occasionally mock trials - contact them for more info)

You can also search Google for "surrogate jury" "mock trial", "virtual juror", "jury focus group" "online juror" + your city to find opportunities in your area.

Indeed and **FlexJobs** also frequently have listings.

Focus Groups

Focus groups are different from surveys in that they are much more in-depth, often require in-person or at least phone/webcam participation and as a result also pay much better.

While surveys mostly involve ticking of questions, focus groups want you to share your opinions, participate in discussion and share your thoughts - often in person (=> higher pay).

Focus groups are a lot more stringent about the target demographic they require and - as is customary in the survey/user testing industry - they usually limit the amount of panels you can participate on per year. So it's best to register with several companies to get frequent offers.

To find current listings from legitimate focus groups and avoid the scammers that you might see on Craigslist and similar sites, you can use this resource:

FindFocusGroups

In addition, here is a comprehensive list of reputable market research companies with active focus groups:

FocusGroup.com
20/20 Research
Respondent.io
Mindswarms
Brand Institute
Nichols Research
Adler Weiner Research
Atkins Research Global
Consumer Opinion Services
Field Work
Probe Market
Focus Scope
Mediabarn Research
Focus Room
Athena Research

You can also search Google for "focus group" + your city to find opportunities in your area. Same with the typical job boards.

To give you a sense of pay range, here are a few examples:

20/20 Research

Their registration site indicates that you can earn $50, 100, $150, or even more per event.

Mindswarms

Most studies pay $50 each (paid within 24 hours)

FocusGroup.com

$60 for a 45-minute focus group on appliances

$65 for a cereal taste test

$75 for a focus group on children's active wear

Focuscope

Between $50 and $250 per opportunity, the average per study is $100.

The above examples all require US residency. However, there are focus groups in almost every country, so just google "focus group" and your city/region and you should find a number of options to start with.

Microtasking

Microtask platforms connect companies who need small tasks completed - so-called "Short Task" - with remote freelance workers who can perform them whenever they have some free time (no minimum hours or specific schedule). Crowdsourcing basically.

The tasks are simple and can be completed in a few minutes. Pay is not great, but they are easy to do on the side and are sometimes quite fun.

Below are the best known platforms:

Amazon Mechanical Turk (mTurk)
Owned by Amazon and one of the most respected microtask platforms. Tasks are called "HIT"s and can be surveys, data entry, transcribing short audio clips, helping a company pick out a photo, copying handwritten notes into a form, etc.

Figure Eight
Another favorite. Tasks include simple internet research, data categorization, categorize social media, moderate content, transcribe audio, draw boxes around images

Clickworker

Tasks include: creating articles or product descriptions on a given topic, proofreading, web research, surveys, categorize data, make short audios & videos with your phone, mystery photography *(similar to mystery shopping)*, app testing

Microworkers

Surveys, data mining, image + video transcription, content moderation, App testing, and many more.

Local Microtasks

Under the motto *"Get paid to shop, eat, and explore in your city"*, these 3 apps let you perform simple tasks in your local area. Everything is done on your phone. Tasks include: visiting stores and taking photos of products or store displays or check prices.

Field Agent
EasyShift
GigWalk

Test Websites & Apps

Website or App testing is an easy way to make some extra money. No special skills required. You just need a computer or smartphone with an in-built microphone and you are good to go. The process is simple: You sign up, take a short test and answer a few demographics questions. That way the platforms can match you with the required target audience for each test.

Why user testing?

Developers and businesses need their websites and apps tested by every day users, so they upload a testing gig to one of the below platforms.

Once your registration is approved, you will either get notified via email of any new tests for your demographic - or - you log in daily to each platform and check for available tests.

Tips that are frequently mentioned by successful user testers:

- *Be thorough in your application and screener test. Your responses will decide whether you get accepted and also what tests you can qualify for.*

- *Be among the first to respond to job emails as they fill up quickly.*

How do you test?

To complete a job, you start running the company's screen capture recording software on your computer *(don't worry, easy-to-do and instructions will be provided)*, follow the instructions and give feedback via your computer's microphone when prompted.

Most jobs pay about $10 per test and take roughly 20 minutes to complete, so not too bad. However, they usually have a weekly limit of how many tests you may complete per week. A simple workaround is to sign up to a number of different platforms, so you can always find available gigs.

Here are some well known options:

uTest
UserTesting
Validately

IntelliZoom
TestingTime
Userzoom
WhatUsersDo
Userlytics
TryMyUI
UserFeel
UserInput.IO
UserCrowd
Analysia
StarUpLift
Enroll
Erli Bird

Rate Ads & Google Search Results

Say *wha*...?

Yep, you can get paid as an "Ad rater" and "Search Engine Evaluator".

Meaning, you review search results (= the list of results that comes up when you "Google" a phrase and hit "Enter"). You will give feedback of whether the results that come up, are suitable and the best possible option for that search phrase to improve user experience.

It's a very popular gig with flexible hours and decent pay - and usually available worldwide. Hours can be limited and are often project based. You have to sign a strict NDA and you are usually not allowed to sign with any competitors.

You don't need any special skills, but should be up to date on current events and trends, plus, all companies will have you go through an extensive test before accepting you (they will provide you prep material that you can even use while completing the test, so not too difficult).

Here are several platforms where you can apply for this gig:

Appen
Lionbridge
iSoftStone *(also other languages)*
ZeroChaos *(occasionally hire ad evaluators)*
KarmaHub *(occasionally have "internet analyst" positions)*

Virtual Customer Support

Virtual Chat Agent

Chat Support positions are very popular, so competition is high.

You need fast typing skills (65+ words per minute) and excellent grammar, punctuation and spelling. Multitasking is another key skill as you will often chat with 3-4 customers at the same time - and sometimes not even from the same company!

Bilingual skills are a plus.

Most positions pay for the minutes you are actually chatting with a customer, not per hour.

The following companies offer chat support positions:

SiteStaff
The Chat Shop
Apple
Wayfair

Uber
FlexJob
Upwork
Ginger.io - *mental health coaches*

❋ ❋ ❋ ❋ ❋ ❋ ❋

Virtual Phone Support

Before you say: *"Absolutely NOT!!"* - please read on... :)

While phone support might not be your dream job, it is one of the easiest ways to generate *immediate* and *consistent* income!

There a more jobs available in this industry than in any other and most come with training and a consistent, regular schedule.

Thanks to modern technology, it has become easy for companies to connect their support calls to private landlines or even your computer.

Pay is around $10-15 per hour and most companies require a minimum time commitment. Evenings/nights and weekends are especially difficult for companies to fill, so you can even start while working a full time job.

Tasks can be very different depending on the company:

- *Set appointments*
- *Talk to people about political issues*
- *Tech Support*
- *Sales Support*
- *Consumer interviews for market research*
- *Telemarketing*
- *Data Collection*
- *Surveys*

You need a newer computer, high-speed internet, a landline and excellent people skills.

Here are some good companies to get you started:

BlueZebra
Appointment setters. $15-$25 per hour. Regular pay raises based on performance

MaritzCX

Collect customer feedback on client products and services - search for "Market Research Interviewer". Minimum 20 hours with some weekends required.

Brighten Communications

Appointment setting, lead generation, market research, database generation

YardiMatrix

Ideal if you have kids at home, as they don't mind some background noise. You will be calling apartment complexes posing as a potential renter to gather information. Positions are seasonal and temporary.

WorkingSolutions

Well known and trusted company in the customer service industry. Not hiring in California, New York, Pennsylvania and Washington.

NexRep

Wide range from travel, to food delivery, non-profits, roadside assistance, retail and more

Nextwave Advocacy

Outbound political calls *(also have letter writing positions to political representatives on behalf of the caller)*

OnPoint@Home
Same as Nextwave

Westat
Data Collection interviews on topics like education, health, transportation, environment. Most positions require you to work nights and weekends and minimum of 20 hours per week.

Pleio GoodStart Mentors
Help patients establish a good medication routine by providing resources and phone reminders.

ParaMeds
Call medical facilities to request patient records. Search for "Remote Records Retrieval Specialists"

Apptical
Phone interviews with insurance agents and their applicants. Medical or insurance background preferred.

VoiceLog
Third-party phone verification

More options:

Amazon
American Express
Hilton
U-Haul
Enterprise

Sutherland CloudSource
Alorica
ACD Direct
Appen
Asurion *(Tech)*
Aspire Lifestyle *(Concierge)*
LiveOps
Sedwick
Kelly Connect
Intuit
Sykes
TTEC

Simple Online Research

In the *Paid Expert* chapter we will cover professional online research gigs, but even without special expertise, you can earn some extra cash with basic research gigs:

Hobby Jam
Simple tasks like giving a 1-line summary on Google search results.

More Online Research gigs through **Microtask sites** and the usual **remote job boards**:

❀ ❀ ❀ ❀ ❀ ❀ ❀ ❀

Court Research *(no prior experience required)*

A popular sub segment among research gigs. Doesn't require any special skills or prior experience. You will go to local courthouses in your area and look up court documents for law firms and other clients. Then, you simply enter them into pre-designed excel sheets or software provided by the client.

Again, no experience required. Pay is per approved document, so will increase as you get more experienced and more skilled at locating documents quickly. *See more detailed info here.*

IT-Boss Research
JBS Court Research Services

Paid Surveys

Paid surveys won't replace a full time job, but can be a nice extra income stream - and fun to do. Most surveys are paid with either gift cards to top retailers - or - "Paypal cash", meaning your earnings will be sent to your Paypal account (not via check or direct deposit). Be sure to check payout times as they can vary greatly - from 2-3 days to 4-6 weeks.

Here are some of the better known companies. Unless otherwise noted, they all offer a choice between gift cards or Paypal cash:

Vindale Research
SurveyJunkie
Swagbucks
Opinion Outpost
YouGov - *Political*
American Consumer Opinion
E-Poll - *Entertainment & Sports*
Toluna
Paid Viewpoint - *Cash only*
Panel Champ - *Cash only*
Baker Street Solutions - *Cash only*

One Opinion
Opinion World
Crowdology
Survey Gizmo
VoxPopMe - *Smartphone App*

Google Opinion Rewards

To participate, you allow Google to install so-called "meters" on your devices that share your internet and TV activity with Google. You need to be a frequent user of both. Pays in gift certificates, not cash.

Pick Brand Names & Slogans

Yes, you can earn cash for picking winning names for brands or web domains. It works similar to design contests like 99 Designs, except that here you come up with cool:

- *Brand or Product Names*
- *Slogans*
- *Logo Designs*
- *Domain names*

If your name is chosen as the winner, you get paid.

Fun, right?

Here are some platforms where you can submit:

Brand/Product Names/SlogansLogos:
SquadHelp

Web Domain Names:
PickyDomains
NamingForce

Happy naming… :)

Data Entry

Data entry is also offered on microtasking platforms, so there is some overlap, but here are a few companies that are more specialized on it.

Pay is usually pretty low, but gigs can easily be done on the side, so one more option for quick cash when you need it. Here are some companies that are occasionally hiring:

The Smart Crowd
SigTrack
Cass Information Systems
Clickworker
Intuit
DionData
Xerox
TTEC
FlexJobs

Intermediate Skills

Movie Captioner & Transcriptions

In case you are wondering: "Captions" are the black sub titles at the bottom of your TV screen that come on when you mute the sound. More importantly, closed captions were created for the hearing impaired.

Someone obviously needs to write them and if you are a fast and accurate typist, this could be you. Meaning, you could enjoy watching movies and TV shows while earning money at the same time!

The following companies hire specifically for TV/Film captioning jobs - and they are quite well paid. You obviously need to type very fast and accurately and meet some basic technical requirements (check each site specifically):

TransPerfect
CaptionMax
Rev

Many companies also hire through the regular job boards - Glassdoor, FlexJobs, Indeed, etc., so check those as well.

Scoping

What is *that*.....?!

As a scopist you edit transcripts from court reporters that were typed on a steno machine and then transcribed to English with a software.

You read for correct syntax, punctuation, missing words etc. - and, of course, accuracy.

A scopist needs to be able to read steno text, understand legal terminology, how to format a transcript and type fast, as you are paid by page.

Pay rates start at around $20 per hour (depending on scopist speed and complexity of the material) all the way up to $35/hour - for rush orders even $50/hour.

This gig definitely requires some specialized training and this free intro course can get you started and give you a better understanding of how it all works and what you need to do:

Free Intro Course(*)

Transcriptions

The prior two chapters focused on specific sub niches in the vast transcription arena. This chapter will look more at General Transcription.

Overall, transcription falls into three different groups:

- General Transcription

- Legal Transcription

*- Medical Transcription (covered in the **Medical Chapter**)*

You obviously need fast, accurate typing skills and a fast, reliable internet connection. In addition, ***Express Scribe Software*** can help make the transcription process a lot faster and easier and eliminate the use of a mouse.

The following companies hire newbies with no experience though they will usually do an evaluation test. If you speak a foreign language, higher earnings are possible:

TransribeMe
Rev
Tigerfish
BabbleType
Accutran Global
CastingWords Workshop
Scribie
Speechpad
Hollywood Transcriptions
Transcript Divas
Ubiqus
GoTranscript
Crowdsurf
Birch Creek

If you want to turn transcription into a more serious career and not just a side gig, you can get some free starter training with these two mini courses:

Free General Transcription Mini-Course(*)
Free Legal Transcription Mini-Course(*)

Proofreading

If you have excellent grammar and punctuation, and an eye for detail, you could start a proofreading career by offering your services to self-publishing authors, which is a booming industry. To get repeat bookings, try to connect with a successful author that frequently publishes a new book and - most importantly - has an active pool of author students who will also need proofreaders on an ongoing basis.

To start getting orders, you could offer that author a free proofread on their next book - or highly discounted. If they liked working with you, there is a good chance, they might recommend you to all their students => continuous flow of work.

Proofreading is different from editing though editors often do both. Editing is more content and structure related whereas proofreading focuses on spelling and grammatical errors, punctuation, missing words, etc.

Beyond authors, the following sites work with freelance proofreaders. Of course, you can also list yourself on Upwork and check listings on FlexJob:

EditFast
Gramlee
Wordvice
ProofreadingServices
Scribendi

While there is no formal course or certificate for proofreading, getting some training certainly doesn't hurt and for starters, you can check out this free training video:

Free Proofread Intro Training(*)

Teach your Passion

Unlike most tutoring sites that thoroughly vet potential teachers,

Superprof

allows anyone to list a skill they can teach or a passion they want to share.

The sign up process is simple, you can set your own rates and then prospective students can get in touch with you.

The platform currently has 7+ million tutors and just as many students.

Review New Music

Playlist Push is an innovative platform that connects up and coming indie musicians with popular playlist curators on Spotify, Apple Music and Deezer.

"Popular" is defined as:

- *Minimum 400 followers per playlist*
- *Minimum 20 active monthly listeners per playlist*
- *Minimum 1% active monthly listeners per playlist*

Playlist Push is very strict with abusers (fake followers, bots and follow gates) and does not accept the following playlist types:

- *Movie/TV series soundtrack playlists*
- *Playlists that frequently change their name to attract followers*
- *Playlists for a specific album, artist or band*

As a playlist owner you get paid to review new songs on Playlist Push. Depending on your reputation and engagement up to $12 per review. You are encouraged to add the songs you liked to your playlist, but it's not required. You are paid as a reviewer.

Indie musicians pay a fee to have their songs reviewed, hoping to get more exposure in popular playlists and peer feedback while curators get paid to find new music for their playlists. Pretty awesome concept!

To help you build a playlist, you can use **Playlist.ne**t and also browse Top 100 Songs in your genre to know what's currently trending and likely to attract a following.

As for getting 400+ followers, here are a few things you can do:

- *Create a social media page for your playlist(s) and build a following*
- *Link to your playlist from this Sub Reddit "**Spotify Playlists**".*
- *This can result in immediate organic traffic and they also hold regular playlist competitions.*
- *Use Spotify's "**Playlist Exchange**" forum*
- *Network with other playlist curators for mutual shoutouts*
- *Network with influencers for shoutouts*

Virtual Assistant

Becoming a "Virtual Assistant (VA)" is one of the easiest entries into the world of home-based jobs and business options, because almost any skill can be monetized as a VA. The most typical tasks are:

- *Secretarial*
- *Receptionist*
- *Social Media Management*
- *Travel arrangements*
- *Research*
- *Bookkeeping*
- *Transcription*
- *Microtasks*

and many more.

For a list of over 150 VA niches, click here(*).

To get started, you can apply to any of the below agencies to get placed on current jobs. Pay will be lower, but you don't have to worry about marketing.

VA AGENCIES

Fancy Hands
Boldly
Contemporary VA
Virtual Gal Friday
VA Sumo
Belay
StartUps Co
99 Dollar Social
Vicky Virtual
Red Butler

If you like the work, flexibility and time freedom that VA freelancing provides, you will want to eventually build your own VA business for much higher earnings, e.g., monthly retainers with long term clients.

For a first introduction to starting your own VA business, you can check out this free training:

Free Training:
***"Breaking into Virtual Assistant Work
The Why, When & How"(*)***

If you already have some VA experience, but want to take things to the next level, Horkey Handbook offers a number of excellent courses and resources, also into more specialize areas like **Project Management, Real Estate, Email Marketing**, starting your own **VA Agency** as well as their flagship VA **Course for Beginners**:

VA Courses(*)

Pinterest VA:

A highly lucrative specialty for VAs is Pinterest. Businesses will pay high monthly retainers for a Ninja VA that can generate them a lot of free traffic from Pinterest (and by extension, Google, as successful pins also usually show on page 1 in Google).

If you love beautiful visuals and working on a classy platform that caters to retail stores, bloggers and eCommerce, becoming a Pinterest VA could be a great fit.

Here is a blog post with more info:

How to Become a Pinterest VA(*)

Fiverr Gigs

$5 bucks per gig may not sound like much, but people have built million dollar businesses from those $5 bucks - and it's a pretty easy entry point!

What am I talking about?

You are probably familiar with **Fiverr** *(if not, it's high time...)*.

Fiverr is, of course, only one of many micro gig platforms where you can list your services and reach customers around the world.

"But I don't have any skills or services to offer..." you might say.

And that's where you are wrong.

Most Fiverr gigs are very basic and those are usually also the most sought after.

For example:

Making the background of a photo transparent, so the object or person in that image can be placed onto another image or background.

I get it. You are not a photoshop ninja, but...

1. You don't need photoshop. There are several free tools available (just google "make background transparent" and pick one). **ClippingMagic** is a low fee tool that makes it super easy - takes only a minute per gig.

2. Photoshop is only $9.99 per month if you were to consider it

3. Learning the basics of Photoshop (and that's all you would need for this and various other micro gigs) can easily be done with a quickie course on Skillshare (first 2 months are free!) - or plenty of Youtube videos to choose from.

See where I'm going...?

We are talking simple gigs that are needed by millions of people every day. Pick a few, list them and start earning money.

Most of these skills can be learned in a day - or be performed by an easy-to-use software taking you only 1-5 minutes to complete.

But you are making $5 for those 5 minutes!

To get ideas, browse the top rated gigs in a field that interests you.

What are the gigs that people are most buying, and is there one you could easily start?

It's best to follow what already works in the beginning as pretty much every gig has already been tried. Don't worry about competition.

Initially, offer free or highly discounted gigs, so you get reviews. Or give a free add-on. In other words, make an irrefusable offer, so customers will choose you, the newbie, over more established sellers with hundreds of reviews.

Go to Facebook groups where your target audience hangs out and offer free coupons there as well.

It's not difficult to get reviews that way and that together with accumulating your first orders, will help you move up the rankings on Fiverr or other platforms, so your gig shows up when people search (="organic" traffic). You need to create buzz around your listing, so Fiverr takes notice and starts showing you to potential customers. Then you build from there.

Here is a free, in-depth course from a 7-figure gig seller - and founder of **Legiit(*)** - on how to build a successful business on gig platforms (not just Legiit):

FREE Course:
Legiit Freelancing Mastery

Beyond **Fiverr** and **Legiit**, you can also list yourself on:

People per Hour
Upwork
Facebook Marketplace

You are welcome to share your first gig in the SassyZenGirl Facebook group for some initial sales and possibly reviews. And you can also ask the group what type of gig they would find helpful and would buy from you.

PRO Skills

Virtual Expert

If you can prove your expertise in a specific area, you can work for several online platforms answering customer questions and completing research assignments.

Ask Wonder

A popular platform where you can complete research assignments for online customers. These usually take 15-20 minutes and pay varies depending on the assignment. (Customers set the fees and you can choose which assignments you accept and when). The company website claims that some of their researchers earn $2,000 per month.

Just Answer

Highly reviewed by Entrepreneur and Forbes. Accepts experts in 75 different specialties. You have to prove your credentials with diplomas, licenses, etc. After that you can set your own hours and mark yourself as available whenever you want to work. The company wants to provide answers within minutes whenever a customer asks a question and will assign the best suited expert that is available at that time. You respond to the customer via chat or phone. Fee is split with "Just Answer".

Maven

As a "Micro-consultant" you set your own rate. When the system finds a match for your expertise, they will contact you. Respond to written questions, talk on the phone or participate in bigger projects.

Clarity

A phone-based platform. Customers choose an expert that best fits their needs and then schedule a consultation. To complete the booking, they pre-pay based on the expert's per-minute-rate and expected length of the call.

Study Pool

On this site you help customers with their homework. They post their question and price range and experts can bid to be selected. Requires a college degree or currently attending college.

Ingenio

Owns four different platforms where you can list yourself as an expert advisor, paid by the minute (your own rates):

• Psychic Advice - **Keen.com** & **PsychicCenter.com**

- Life Coaching - **LifeAdvice.com**
- Anything under the Sun - **Ether.com**

PrestoExperts

Answer customer questions via chat, phone or email. Create a profile and set your own rates.

6ya

Interesting option, offering a wider range of expert areas from computer help to car advice, plumbing and DIY/Home Improvement, animal communication and sports advice. Calls usually last around 5 minutes and you get paid per call at the rate you set.

This platform also works well if you have a following on social media, Youtube, podcast or blog. This way, you can offer your followers to get their questions answers on a quick - paid - call.

You accept calls through a smartphone app whenever you want to be available, so your phone number remains private.

Operator

Phone app that helps shoppers find what they are looking for. You consult with the customer and then purchase and ship the products for them using their credit card *(stored securely online with Operator)*.

Virtual Tech Support

Same as before, but specialized on tech support:

6ya
See prior chapter.

Geeks.online
Both remote and onsite computer repair and service

PlumChoice
Largest remote tech support provide in the US

Apple
Hires remote tech support for their products. Need 2+ years of troubleshooting experience.

Best Buy
Same as Apple. Hires for their "Geek Squad".

Xerox
Employs a whopping 8,000+ remote workers, not just for tech support, but also customer care, data entry, image tagging, quality control, admin support, systems development & software programming.

Virtual Consultant

Freelance consulting gigs can be highly lucrative and the below platforms connect virtual experts with companies around the world. Applicants are thoroughly vetted and need to provide credentials and relevant experience top be considered for suitable projects:

On Frontiers

Connects experts with clients around the world. Promises *"Experts on any topic, in any market, in under 48 hours"*. Clients can set up any of the following four options:

- *Phone consultations*
- *Contracts for short and long term consulting*
- *Ongoing advisor or Board member*
- *Permanent Hire*

You set your own rates and schedule.

10EQS

Connects experts with mostly professional services companies around the world. Virtual global network of 1,000 specialized consultants in a variety of fields, ranking from health care to finances, aerospace, automotive, education, legal, chemicals and metals, professional services, telecommunications, logistics and many more.

"We take clients' issues, break them apart find the right specialists for each piece, and put everything back together to provide a complete and customized solution." *(Managing Director Mark Donaldson)*.

You can answer questions for specific projects as an "Industry Expert" *(several hundred dollars for a 1-2 hour interview)* or work as an independent consultant/ collaboration manager for 10EQS *(averaging $1,500 per day)*.

More platforms for independent remote consultants:

Internal Consulting

Expert360

Virtual Teacher

Whatever expertise you have, you can now teach it online to almost anyone in the world - courtesy of the internet.

You can list your services on many different platforms and start teaching via video chat - either one-on-one or groups.

Unlike Academic tutoring which we'll cover a little later, these sites don't usually have any certification requirements though it certainly helps to have some in your profile to attract students.

The following platforms allow you to list yourself, set your own schedule and fees and start earning money as a virtual teacher:

PrestoExperts
TakeLessons
BrainMass
Clarity
Maven
Ether

Translation

If you are fluent in another language - in particular, Spanish, Portuguese, German, Russian or Chinese - you will find plenty of translator gigs.

Jobs could be in customers service, transcriptions, written translations or working as an interpreter.

As an author, I've frequently been contacted by translators or agencies offering to translate my books - either for a flat fee (usually pretty high) or profit sharing. So authors can, once again, be a target market (among many others).

Otherwise, it's easiest to go through an agency in the beginning. Pay is lower, but work is more steady and you don't have to do any marketing.

Here is a list of translation agencies:

WeLocalize
Argos Multilingual
Rev
TeleLanguage

TransPerfect
VerbalizeIt
LanguageLine
Gengo
SDL
Capita
AccuRapid
Translations ABC
Upwork
Guru

Best 100 Companies for Flexible Translation Jobs

College Degree Required

Virtual Academic Tutor

Remote academic tutoring and test prep gigs are available at the following companies *(require college degree and teaching certifications)*:

Tutor
You need to prove extensive training and qualifications and pass a rather challenging test and background check. Student interaction is via a virtual classroom.

Brainfuse
Offers tutoring in 5 different areas: K-12 students, Higher Ed, library patrons of all ages, transition assistance for veterans, and career services (resumes/career guidance). Require Master's Degree and prior teaching experience as well as US residence.

PrepNow
K-12 only. Various subjects, plus SAT, ACT prep. Requires 2+ years teaching experience and a Bachelor's Degree. US based only.

Aim4A

K-12 students. Classes in Math, English, Science as well as TAG. Also, ACT, SAT and TOEFL prep. Bachelor's Degree required. Teaching certificate desirable.

Study Pool

Help customers with their homework. Customers post their question and price range and tutors can bid to be selected. Requires a college degree or currently attending college.

Yup Tutoring

Different from **Study Pool** in that it does *not* allow tutors to answer questions, but rather wants the tutor to guide the student to the answer. This is very strictly enforced. Communication is via online chat. Only math, chemistry and physics.

Test prep:

Kaplan
Pearson

Academic Test Scorer

Another goodie you can do in your PJs, courtesy of the internet.

You don't necessarily need an educational background, but a college degree is required. Most companies will also put you through an assessment test and you will attend an orientation.

You can apply to these companies:

WriteScore
ACT
Measurement Inc.
ETS
Literably
FlexJobs

English Test Scorer

Another scoring gig, but in this case, it's English tests for Japanese students!

Over 500,000 are tested for their English proficiency in Japan every year and Japanese companies eagerly seek English native speakers with college degrees to grade the tests.

Pay is per script rated and comes to around $18-25/h depending on the rater's speed.

Virtual English Tutor

Staying with the *English as a 2nd Language* theme, you can, of course, also teach English online. It'a an industry that has exploded over the last few years, especially with companies based in China.

Pay has also gotten better - with some companies at least - and you get all the time flexibility you could ever want. Just set your availabilities and have the companies do the booking. Usually, they also provide training and teaching materials.

You will need a bachelor's degree for most of them. Not necessarily in teaching though it certainly helps. Here are the best known companies to apply to:

Boxfish

GogoKid

Cambly

italki

VIPKid

QKid

NiceTalk Tutors

Magic Ears

Go Fluent

Education First

PRO Virtual Researcher

There are many ways to get paid for online research, both for simple tasks that only take a few minutes to complete all the way up to professional level research assignments.

First Quarter Finance
Occasional openings for "Remote Research Analysts" to perform consumer related research:
Questions about a store policy, where to buy something, personal finance, budget travel, store services and others. Academic level research requiring solid knowledge of Excel.

10EQS
Occasionally has online researcher openings in addition to their consulting gigs. Business degrees and experience preferred.

RWS
Works as a competition. Once registered, you can submit completed research assignments to "Public Studies". The best submissions get paid. Over time you can earn "Study Expert" designation and may

then qualify for "invitation only" private studies with guaranteed pay (fixed fee or hourly rate).

Ask Wonder

Also listed in a prior chapter, this popular platform lets you take on research assignments from online customers. The company website claims that some of their researchers earn $2,000 per month.

Virtual Lawyer

UpCounsel connects top level virtual attorneys with business owners and companies, incl. giants like AirBnB. The concept is similar to UpWork: Clients post a job and attorneys can submit proposals - at their own rates. The platform handles all monetary transactions and all jobs are rated.

UpCounsel's 5,000+ attorney roster includes Harvard Law graduates, former partners and associates at major law firms and Fortune 500 companies.

If you are an experienced attorney and want to get out of a stressful corporate career while setting your own hours and working from home, this is a great platform:

UpCounsel

I frequently use UpCounsel for my legal business needs *(trademarks, contracts, LLCs, general questions)* and always had excellent results while paying far less than with a regular law firm - yet getting the same quality and experience. This link will give you $100 off, should you choose to work with one of their attorneys:

Hire a best-in-class attorney on UpCounsel and save $100(*)

While UpCounsel features the highest quality lawyers in online legal services and allows you to set your own rates, here are several other (well known) options:

RocketLawyer
LegalZoom
LegalShield

Sell your Lesson Plans

An awesome passive income side gig for teachers. You can upload your lesson plans and worksheets *(that you previously created and already used in your past school year)* to platforms like:

Teachers Pay Teachers

Looks a little like Fiverr for teachers...:) - and quite a brilliant idea.

Go Teachers!

Pro Book Reviewer

Love reading books?

How about getting paid for it? Just for writing a quick 250-300 word review?

That's what the below review services offer!

Kirkus
Booklist
Publisher's Weekly
Online Book Club
US Review of Books
Women's Review of Books
Any Subject Books

You will need to submit writing samples (ideally reviews) as well as other relevant qualifications, literally or otherwise. Each platform has its own set of requirements (college degree is usually one of them), so just read through them and give it a go.

Local Gigs

Attend Movie Premieres

I definitely want *that* job!

Get paid to watch movie premieres? - Sign me up!

What's it all about?

Movie studios and theaters always need info and specific data about premiere audiences:

Patron count, audience reaction, most popular screening times, what previews are shown, feedback on the theatre and concession stands. So they hire independent evaluators to get "in-theater checks". That's where you come in!

Pay can range from $10 to $30, plus, often reimbursement of your tickets and concessions, so a pretty nifty deal, especially, when you had planned on seeing that movie anyway.

To apply you need to fill out an application with **Certified Field Associates**, one of the largest mystery shopping companies.

Fake Patient

I remember from my med school days that we frequently had actors perform as patients during exams. They seemed to enjoy it very much and - made some money on the side.

The official term is "Standardized Patient" and the best way to land those gigs is to contact nearby medical or nursing schools (in any country). You could also try local job boards.

Rent a Friend

I know....sounds ominous, but **RentAFriend** is actually a legit site. And no, it's NOT a dating platform - they are very adamant about that!

Here is how it works:

You can join the site for free and people in need of a +1 can contact you to attend concerts, sporting events, family functions, VIP events and much more.

If you have special skills like dancing, cooking or languages, you can list them - and possibly teach them.

The site is also frequently used by travelers or people new to town who would like a local to show them the area, rather than going with a generic tour bus. As a travel writer, I frequently had locals show me their town and region, and it was always a much nicer experience. Plus, you get a deeper understanding of what's going on beneath the surface. How people think, local issues, etc. - I remember that especially vividly about South Africa.

You can charge up to $50 per hour and set your own schedule. According to the site, full-time "friends" (five days a week) earn up to $2,000 per week(!) though that would probably depend very much on your location.

Local Tasks & Errands

A variety of apps allow you to pick up errands, task and delivery jobs in your local area - whenever you have free time. Often quite well paid.

Gigs can include odd jobs around the house or office, assembling furniture, carry groceries up a flight of stairs, checking things out for out-of-towners and the various delivery and shopping gigs **that we'll look at in the CAR CHAPTER**.

GENERAL TASKS & HANDYMAN

Care
TaskRabbit
Gigs include: handyman, cleaning, delivery, moving, furniture assembly, personal assistant.

LOCAL MICROTASKS

Under the motto *"Get paid to shop, eat, and explore in your city"*, these 3 apps let you perform simple tasks in your local area. Everything is done on your phone. Tasks include: visiting stores and taking photos of products or store displays or check prices.

Field Agent
EasyShift
Gigwalk

Flexible Shift Work

If you are looking for flexible shift work in hospitality, event staff, delivery, retail or warehousing, there are several apps that can quickly connect you to local companies.

Wonolo
ShiftGig

These two apps connect available workers with "shifts" at restaurants, bars, music and sports events, conventions, retail stores or warehouses.

You only work when you want to.

To get added to the roster, you need to fill out an application and upload your resume. ShiftGig partners with local staffing services who will conduct an in-person interview to qualify you for the type of work you will have access to. Wonolo interviews over the phone.

Once accepted, you can access available gigs through the smartphone app and apply. Workers are rated at the end of each shift, so it's important to do an excellent job each time. Payout is via direct deposit the following Friday (Shiftgig) or the following day (Wonolo).

Wonolo lists the following hourly pay ranges on their blog:

$10-$16 for warehousing/order fulfillment
$15-$35 for delivery jobs
$15-$25 for general labor/moving jobs
$13-$30 for brand ambassador and event staffing

Handyman & Cleaners

Contractors and mechanics often have long wait times, leaving customers desperate for someone who is available right away to fix minor problems.

These two sites can connect you with potential customers for both handyman and cleaning gigs:

Handy
TaskRabbit

Two more platforms for cleaners:
MaidSimple
HouseKeeper

Lawn services and yard work:
TaskEasy

As a contractor, you can also get yourself listed with local referral networks - if there are some in your area. More on those in the business chapter.

Mobile Car Mechanic

Car mechanics who make house calls!

Every car owner's dream!

If you have solid experience with basic repair and maintenance, you can start your own mobile mechanic business in your neighborhood.

You could even throw in a mobile car wash option and owners will absolutely love you - I would...:)

If you don't want to deal with marketing and basically just start tomorrow, **YourMechanic** is an awesome app that will allow you to do just that.

With the irresistible tagline: *"Imagine if you never had to deal with an auto shop again",* **YourMechanic** has grown a vast network of car mechanics in 2,000 cities nationwide who make house calls to your office or home!

They only do basic repair and maintenance.

Once you've signed up, you can choose your own schedule, enter it into the app, and *YourMechanic* gets to work and books you with car owners in your area.

Pay is between $40-60 per hour according to their website.

＊＊＊＊＊＊＊＊＊＊

Car Inspections for Remote Clients

If you are car expert, you can also perform car inspections for remote buyers with **We Go Look** - a professional fields services platform.

Phone Consultations for Remote Clients

And you can offer to consult customers via phone through a platform called **6ya**. Calls usually last around 5 minutes and you get paid per call at the rate you set.
You accept calls through a smartphone app whenever you want to be available, so your phone number remains private.

Inspect Homes & Cars for Remote Buyers

We Go Look does not just offer car inspections for out-of-towners, but also gigs for home inspectors, notaries and even pickups/deliveries.

If your expertise lies in real estate, you can scout properties for potential out-of-town buyers while keeping the freedom of a flexible schedule and being your own boss.

Professional Field Services
for remote buyers + companies

We Go Look

Inspections *(vehicles, homes, equipment)*
Documents *(signing, pick-up, notary)*
Assessment
Pickup & Delivery

Mystery Shopping

A nice gig to make some extra money - both online and in-person. There are plenty of offers as companies are always short of secret shoppers and some are paid quite well *(Example: visit a car dealership, pretend to buy a car, incl. test drive - $60)*.

What is "Mystery Shopping"?

You basically pose as a real customer and provide feedback to the company on your shopping experience, the customer service you received, appearance of the store etc. In return, the company pays you a fee and reimburses you for any purchases they asked you to make.

Some jobs are strictly from home: You either test/ evaluate a website or online shopping platform, or you make test calls to evaluate customer service for a company *(Example: $3-5 per call, taking about a minute each)*.

Store assignments usually entail a a list of tasks to complete, such as buying a specific product or test a service. Afterwards, you report back on the store's performance. Layout, cleanliness, staff, etc.

Typical gigs include:

- *Car Dealerships*
- *Salons*
- *Restaurants*
- *Electronic stores like Best Buy*
- *Movie Theaters*
- *Makeup counters*
- *Clothing stores*

As for income potential: it depends on how much time you can put in and how well gigs in your area are paid. Rural areas often pay better, because there are far fewer shoppers.

Real life examples:
- One guy made $14,000 in one year, just doing assignments on the weekends and during his lunch break.
- Another women made up to $5,000 in one month though her regular intake was more around $400-500 per month.

Income depends on various factor, but decent earning potential is there - if mostly on a part time basis.

Beware of the many scams in this field!

For example, _**don't ever pay**_ a sign up fee or pay to see job listings - and always check if the company is listed with the **MSPA)**

Mystery shopping or "Secret shopping" is a legitimate gig and will never go out of demand as companies will always need real life feedback to improve their services.

This also applies internationally. While most of the companies listed below are US based, you can Google in your country and will probably find plenty of options there as well.

Here are a number of reputable companies you can sign up with:

Bestmark
Sinclair Customer Metrics
Market Force
Secret Shopper
GWB

Pinnacle
A Closer Look
Perception Strategies
FieldAgent
Ipsos *(also international)*

MYSTERY SHOPPING BY PHONE
(from home)
Call Center QA
ARC Consulting
Yardi Matrix
Intellicheck

Yelp Community Ambassador

This one's not for introverts, but if you love hosting local events and connecting with people, becoming a local community ambassador for Yelp might be for you.

You will organize events from your home office and need to be well connected in your community. If you are outgoing and a go-getter, this can be a great fit when they need someone in your area.

Your Home

You might not realize how many options you have to monetize your home - and I'm not just talking about AirBnB...

Let's have a look:

Micro-Restaurant

You can turn your home into a "micro restaurant" for a night and host travelers from around the world who love meeting locals and learning about different cuisines.

The following sites make it easy to connect - and get paid for your passion - while meeting interesting people and making new friends. You can also offer cooking classes and food tours to your favorite local foodie hotspots:

EatWith
Eat At A Locals
EatAway
BonAppetour
CookApp
CoLunching
MealSharing
ChefsFeedExperiences

Offer Cooking Classes:
Cookly

Micro-Hotel

AirBnB is, of course, the most famous option for renting a room in your home at hotel prices. But there are quite a few more:

VRBO
HomeAway
Wimdu *(City Apartments)*
FlipKey
HomeStay
VillasDirect
OneFineStay *(Luxury)*
Sublet

Host RVs & Campers

If you have a large backyard or driveway, you can host RVs or Campers:

CampSpace
RVwithMe

Rent Parking Spots

You can also rent out your driveway as parking space, especially if you live near attractions or convention centers where parking can be sparse. This can also work if your condo comes with a designated parking spot that you never use:

Just Park
MoneyParking

Or... just put up a "Parking" sign outside your driveway.

Rent Storage Space

Yep, there is even app to rent out storage space in your house:

Store at My House

Pet Day Care

Will be covered in the **PET CHAPTER**.

Kids Day Care

If you are great with kids and are currently raising small kids of your own, a day care center in your home could be another fun "work from home" option.

Aside from posting in your local neighborhood and networking with employers, you can connect with parents via the below sites. Several have "child care center" options, and even on a regular babysitting site, you can meet - and impress - potential clients who are actively looking and might be interested in a more permanent solution:

Care
SitterCity
Care4Hire
Seeking Sitters
UrbanSitter

Cash your Trash

How about making some cash with stuff you would have thrown out anyway?

Here are some of the many throw-away items that you can "monetize":

Your Junk Mail
The **Small Business Knowledge Center** will pay you for your junk mail. Amazing, right...?
All you have to do is **sign up**, and then send them your junk mail every week in a pre-paid envelope.
Has to be related to finance, insurance, telecommunications or travel. For every piece of mail you earn points that can be redeemed for cash.
US Monitor provides a similar service.

Your used Cooking Oil
White Mountain Biodiesel will pick up your used cooking oil and turn it into biodiesel - how cool is *that*? They are constantly expanding their territory, but even if they don't yet have a route near you, you can google your region and will probably find a similar company nearby.

Your unused *(unwanted)* Gift Cards

All those free gift cards for stores you never use...? - This is where you can cash them. Just enter the card's barcode, get a quote and send them to:

Cardpool
Giftcard Granny

Used Makeup

Bought the wrong color, but don't want to throw it away. Then sell your makeup on these platforms:

Glambot
Muabs

Your Receipts

The following apps use customer receipts for market research and will pay you for every receipt you scan in *(no kidding!)*:

Receipt Hog
Ibotta
Checkout 51

Your Printer Cartridges

Evolve Recycling will buy your used printer cartridges.

Your used Electronics
Green Buyback
Gazelle
usell
YouRenew

Your Scrap Metal
GotScrap

Your Wood *(and even ashes)*
Antiques Beams and Boards

Your Cardboard Boxes
Boxcycle

Old Books
Cash 4 Books

Old Jewelry
Out of your Life

Your Car

Deliveries

In addition to the errand and small task options in the **LOCAL GIGS Chapter**, let's now look specifically at delivery gigs with your car (and in some cases, bike):

Grocery Shopping
Can be combined with your own grocery shopping.
Shipt
Instacart
Burpy
Favor *(Texas)*

Restaurant Take-out Deliveries
Doordash
UberEats

General Deliveries
Also via bicycle and on foot.
Postmates
Amazon Flex
(Amazon Prime Products)
TaskRabbit

Help Folks Move

The following apps allow you to pick up moving jobs with your truck or van - large cars or SUVs are also eligible. This can include transporting items, helping people move, hauling away junk, picking up larger orders.

GoShare
BuddyTruk
Dolly

Even if you don't have a car you can make some money as a moving assistant with:

Bellhops

Beyon∂ UBER...

Of course, you can also use your car as a local taxi - and there is more than just **Uber** and **Lyft**:

Drive Patients & Caregivers
UberHealth
Lyft Concierge

Health Care, Seniors, Businesses. Driver sign up via the regular **Lyft** portal, but Concierge customers need to have a business account.

Drive Kids
Zum
HopSkipDrive

The UBER for Kids and Schools
Currently offers a promotion for new ∂rivers:
$1,000 guaranteed the 1st month after 40 ri∂es in 30 ∂ays

Drive Seniors
SilverRide

(San Francisco - Kansas City)
The UBER for Seniors

Lyft & **Uber**
have partnered with the AARP to increase senior
mobility, offering courses for seniors nationwide
teaching them to book rides via smartphone.

Lyft also offers **Lyft Concierge** where caregivers can
book rides for seniors.

Freedom in Motion
Florida based UBER partnership for seniors.

Via
Local shuttle frequently used by seniors.
(New York - Washington DC - Chicago)

Ridesharing Shuttles

Via
(New York - Washington DC - Chicago)

Ads on Your Car

"Carvertising" can offer some easy passive income, but you have to be careful to only sign up with legitimate companies (quite a few scams around).

Legit companies will:

- Not ask you for money
- Ask about your car and driving habits *(the more you drive, the better your chances)*
- Require you to have car insurance
- Have a real business address on their website *(not just a contact form)*

Here are a few examples:

Carvertise
Pay Me For Driving
Wrappify

Getting these gigs is very competitive and mostly available in bigger cities to frequent drivers.

You will have a better chance when you work for Uber or any of the aforementioned delivery and ride-hailing services since advertisers want to see lots of driving hours in busy areas.

Being part of a ride-sharing service would also get you access to in-car "entertainment", the little TV screens you might have seen in taxis with local news, announcements and ads. Several companies partner specifically with individual ride-hailing drivers:

Vugo
Viewdify
Firefly

Rent out your Car

Just like AirBnB, most Western countries now also have P2P services for car rentals. You can book them just like you would on AirBnB.

A newer addition (in the US) is **GetAround**(*). This service not only connects renters and car owners, but also provides:

• *Protection for your car*
• *Screens all potential drivers and*
• *Offers technology for remote access to your car via phone*

They also:

• *Enforce non smoking rules and*
• *Mileage limits*
• *Cover insurance and help with repairs and out time if needed*

Their app GetAround Connect™ allows renters to locate and unlock your car (so you don't have to be there in person). Not only that, it also adds security features like GPS tracking, tamper detection, and engine lock.

You receive a Digital Key, so you always know where your car is parked and you can lock/unlock remotely with your phone. They can even set you up with a dedicated parking spot.

Here is another service to list your car:

TravelCar
(incl. free airport parking while you travel)

For international platforms, simply Google "Peer-to-peer Car rental services" in your country. You can also find an extensive list in my **TRAVEL for FREE book**:

Home-Based Business Ideas

Referral Business

A contractor referral business can be a lucrative part time gig and is a favorite among stay-at-home moms.

You don't need experience in home improvement or any experience with a referral business.

Instead, you can join a franchise opportunity called the "**Home Referral Network (HRN)**"(*) that has been around for many years and helped hundreds of businesses get started - both in the US *and internationally*.

HRN was, in fact, founded by a Long Island stay-at-home mom and provides in-depth training and ongoing consulting to help newbies get started.

Why contractors?

Because, as any home owner will know, finding quality contractors is difficult. Home owners looking for your help won't be hard to find, no matter where you are, making this business model quite unaffected by economic fluctuations as repairs and home improvement are always needed.

Contractors will be happy to have you connect them with owners without them having to spend their precious time on marketing. In return, they pay you a commission on every job you procure for them.

If marketing scares you, fear not, as HRN provides ample training. This is very much a "word of mouth" business and networking in your local community is key. Given the urgent need for a service like this, a well placed feature in your local newspaper might already open the floodgates.

Most of the work is done from home via phone and computer and earning potential is significant, especially for a part-time business (somewhat dependent on your location, of course). Some in the HRN network are making 10K+ per month.

More info on **HRN's website(*)**.

Home Staging

Home staging is another potentially lucrative part time business that you can start without prior experience - *if* - you have an eye for interior design.

"Home stagers" are hired to make homes look their absolutely best prior to inviting potential buyers. It is an art, and fabulously staged homes can easily gain an additional $10,000 to even $100,000 in sales price!

That's why sellers are willing to pay top dollar to the right professional.

While you don't need a home staging background, a good eye for style and design is certainly necessary. Beyond that, good training can get you started quickly.

Debra Gould is the "Queen of Home Staging" and has run a highly successful training program since 2005. By now 30,000 students in 23 countries have graduated and built home staging businesses in their area.

You can check out her training and much more detailed information at **StagingDiva(*)** (*love* the name!).

Or start with:

Free Home Staging Jumpstart Course(*)

#DecorBoss

Whether you just have an "eye for design" or can boast a full design degree, you can find your place in the lucrative and creative arena of interior design.

You can either build your own customer base, negotiate with vendors, run PR and list yourself on platforms like **Houzz** - or - join a well known franchise network like the:

Decorating Den

...where you can benefit from a pre-established system and extensive training program to start with a bang.

Under the hashtag #DecorBoss, a Decorating Den franchise will provide you with:

- Complete "turn-key" business system
- Ongoing professional training with 1-on-1 coaching
- Complete business set up and client management system

- Wholesale buying network with over 100 national suppliers
- Graphic design & social media team at your disposal
- Professional marketing guru with connections to national outlets
- Turn-key systems for marketing and generating new clients

and much more.

To take a "tour" visit the **Decorating Den.**

Baby Swimming Instructor

A beautiful and much loved home biz opportunity - also available internationally. See more info in the **KIDS CHAPTER.**

Publish Bestsellers

Self-Publishing is the path that made everything possible for me.

Helping me to grow a 6 figure passive income business, going on 7 now.

Allowing me to take off weeks at a time while money is still flowing in.

Growing a large worldwide audience - pretty much on autopilot.

There is no faster, more effective method to growing a following quickly than self-publishing on Amazon with its billion strong audience - *IF* - you learn the secrets of long term, consistent sales and not just a quickie Bestseller that fades soon after launch.

Sadly, that is what happens to most self-published authors, including those who offer expensive courses on publishing... :)

If you want long term success and are serious and ready to rock, I have a fun gift for you:

The Top Selling Publishing Guide - FREE for a short time *(grab it now!):*

BestsellerPublishing.net

You will learn how to successfully launch your first book to Bestseller status (non fiction), just like thousands of other first-time authors around the world, some even outranking famous authors like Tim Ferriss, Napoleon Hill, Hall Elrod and Brian Tracy.

Once you've learned the basics, we can expand into long term sales and growing a following.

Funny Mugs & Tees

This one's fun and very easy to start!

Create funny mugs (or T-Shirts) and sell them on Amazon.

Merch-by-Amazon for T-shirts and hoodies is a well known program and recently expanded to the UK and Germany.

You have to fill out an application and get accepted (not everyone does), and then slowly build up your portfolio through different tiers (more on that in my *passive income book at:* **PassiveIncomeFreedom.com**).

This is called "Print-on-Demand", meaning, you upload designs and Amazon prints and ships them when a customer orders. You don't have to store inventory or deal with customer queries, you just have to market them properly, so they sell.

Selling Funny Mugs!

Another fun option I came across recently is **selling funny mugs** via a platform called Gearbubble. You can sell on Amazon, Etsy, eBay or your Shopify store, and fulfillment is handled by Gearbubble which integrates directly with all the above platforms.

Simple, "ugly" mugs with funny text tend to be the most successful and they are super easy to create - no designer needed.

Rachel Rofe turned this into a 7-figure fully automated business and shares more info in this:

FREE TRAINING:
"Discover how you can make DAILY sales of on-demand products on the world's biggest e-commerce sites without spending ANY money. No ad costs, no outsourcer costs, no risk." (*)

Subscription Boxes

Sounds like a *deliciously* fun idea - also, on the receiving end as a customer!

After all, who wouldn't love getting a gift box every month...?

What's a subscription box business?

You target a specific niche (cat lovers, Star Wars, body products) or a segment of the population (nurses, teachers, etc.) and create monthly gift boxes with a few curated items that will appeal to them. In return they pay you a monthly subscription fee.

To give you some visual examples, you can check out these top selling subscription boxes:

Fandom of the Month
for geeky women who love jewelry and treats

The Butter Box
body products with food flavors like chocolate, honey, vanilla

Cruelty-Free for You & Me

vegan and cruelty free pet and beauty products

You can either start your own website or use a platform like **Cratejoy** with all the necessary backend functionality already in place:

- Storefront
- Customer and transaction management
- Shipping labels

They also have a training platform called: **Subscription School** to help you get started and find subscribers quickly.

You can check out Cratejoy and more info.

Local Marketing Agency
(Remote)

Don't skip this chapter.... :)

Even if you think you weren't "born with a marketing gene" or you are too much of an "introvert" - hold that thought.

Starting a marketing agency is one of the fastest and most lucrative ways to grow a home-based business. Even better, since a lot of the steps and day-to-day can eventually be automated or outsourced to a VA, all five options can turn into more passive income long term, so don't let the "M" word scare you off....

Marketing is not as complicated as you might think, nor is it boring, tedious or sleazy. Definitely much easier than anything you ever learned in college - or even high school.

You got this!

Knowledge is power! You just need to know what to do - step by step - and you will find that it's all a lot easier than you thought, actually quite fun - and well paid!

Good marketing is what can make or break any business and if you can provide a steady flow of new customers, companies will be happy to pay you well, just so you keep that flow going.

We are talking $500-1000 per month, _per_ client - for starters!

Ongoing monthly retainers.

For bigger accounts, certainly more, once you have more experience and glowing testimonials to share.

The key is to focus on ONE platform and become the top marketing expert for that one marketing strategy in your area.

We'll look at:

- **2 Local SEO options (maps & videos)**
- **Facebook Ads**
- **Pinterest**
- **Instagram**

Why local?

Because it's a lot easier to gain traction and connect with the "right" customers - also a lot less competition unless you live in a major metropolis.

Very important: You do *not* have to live in the geographical area you choose, as everything is done online, incl. client communications. Most clients you will probably never meet in person (introverts rejoice... :)!

The two SEO options can easily be combined, though there, too, you first want to start with one, master that, and then add the second.

Down the road, as you get more experienced in SEO, you can also add ranking their website as an additional service to get up to at least $1,000 per month, but for starters, just ranking in the maps - which is *very* easy to do in smaller locations - is a good way to start.

The three social media options should definitely not be combined!

You want to be seen as a specialist. As the master ninja for that particular platform.

That's when companies are willing to pay the big bucks, because they, too, understand that no one can master them all. They are not interested in a jack-of-all-trades, they want the TOP expert in that field.

So, pick either one of the SEOs or one of the social media options. Whichever platform most appeals to you as you will be spending a lot of time there.

The two SEO blueprints are pretty simple, but you should have at least a basic understanding of SEO and what it's all about. If needed, you can **read this little Beginner Guide as an introduction**, so you know the terminology and how it all works.

For the social media options, which have a high earning potential, you *need* to get training from a pro or you will never get anywhere.

A few Youtube videos or blog posts will not cut it in this case. You are learning a new profession and you need to know the ins and outs of that profession. Including - very importantly - the special hacks, the top performers on these platforms use, so you can become one of them.

I'm sharing a low cost training option for each, so you can get started right away. None even remotely what a college education would cost you - and with much higher earning potentials than the 40K-60K a year job that most college grads end up with.

It's important to remember the enormous amounts people are willing to spend on a college degree (US) and what terrible ROI (return of investment) it has for most!

Investing up to 6 figures into obtaining that degree - and 4-6 years of your life(!) - to then make a mere 40-60K a year (the average American income), while burdened with students loans and stuck in a job that most people hate, with minimal vacation time.

Terrible ROI!

Time to change that - let's roll:

Pinterest Agency

Pinterest is an amazing platform for a marketing agency for several reasons:

• Not as oversaturated as Facebook and Instagram

• Google "loves" Pinterest, meaning: well performing pins will also easily rank on page 1 in Google, giving the client even more organic traffic *("organic" = from searches, not ads = free traffic)*

• Over 90% of Pinterest users state that they have used Pinterest to make purchase decisions or straight out purchased right from Pinterest.

• It is the only social media platform where users go to shop and are not annoyed when they see offers. Quite the opposite - that's what many come for.

• Pinterest is huge for eCommerce! = Tons of potential clients.

• It takes far less time to get traction and start ranking than a website in Google

- While progress is initially slow as you build "authority" and a following, successful pins can stay at the top of searches for years to come. Similar to Google or Youtube, but opposite to other social media platforms where posts can go viral temporarily, but then disappear and you have to start all over again. However, while you are growing, many pins will already rank in Google and send traffic to your clients.

- Pinterest audiences as a whole are wealthier, friendlier, more educated and sophisticated than other social media platforms => easier to sell to, including for high ticket items.

To learn how to grow on Pinterest and funnel traffic to a business website or blog, I recommend this course by 2 bloggers who generate 100K+ per month(!) in sales from Pinterest traffic!

PINTEREST TRAFFIC AVALANCHE(*)

Many clients are more interested in having pins rank in Google than Pinterest.

To give you an example: an SEO friend of mine gets paid $4,000 a month to run the Pinterest page for an educational site. They pay him to rank pins and boards in Google, which is very easy to do as I mentioned before, because Google naturally favors Pinterest and will give well-optimized pins extra love and high ranking.

While this is an extreme example, it shows how much earning potential you have with this platform and how well worth it is to invest in good training. Really apply yourself and then monetize - both for your own projects and for high paying clients who will pay you a monthly retainer!

Instagram Agency

Instagram is another big power house in the marketing agency scene.

Most businesses are now aware how powerful Instagram marketing can be and want in on the fun.

Even for something as unlikely as dentists, believe it or not!

I know of one dentist in Melbourne who had developed as special teeth whitening procedure. He offered local celebrities free treatments in return for a shoutout to their Instagram audiences.

It worked like wildfire as many of their followers also wanted teeth whitenings from this same doctor and he soon starting hiring and training additional dentists to cover the many incoming requests.

Eventually, he opened additional locations in Sydney and elsewhere, turning a little teeth whitening project into a 7-figure powerhouse that mostly ran on autopilot.

That's one of many example of how powerful Instagram can be.

To learn the best techniques - and most of all, stay on top of the frequent algorithm updates and changes, check out this free training by Josue Pena who managed IG campaigns for Gary Vaynerchuck and other heavyweights, and turned his Instagram agency into a 7-figure business:

FREE Instagram Training:

"The Weird System That Gets Me 50K Followers A Month AND A $200K Dollar Paycheck…

…without using bots, or fake followers AND how you can easily knock if off in less than 1 Day"

Facebook Ads Agency

Every business wants Facebook traffic. Facebook ads are the most reliable way to generate that traffic consistently and target the ideal audience.

Facebook ads are formidable and as such a little more complicated to learn, plus, they require a higher budget from the client, in addition to your monthly retainer.

They also require more ongoing maintenance from you - which is why your pay should be equally higher!

$1,000 per month is a minimum once you feel comfortable that you can deliver results consistently.

And that's not as difficult as it may seem. Certainly not in a local market.

Get good training, test it out yourself for 3-4 weeks and you are ready to go.

Like is said, marketing is not rocket science, but you need to know the exact steps and special tips - both for running an agency, and to promote your own business projects.

One of the best courses to learn Facebook ads for all kinds of different business types and genres is Kevin David's training. You can check out a free Training Class here and get a sense:

FREE Facebook Ads Masterclass(*)

He built a massive 8 figure business with online courses and various ecommerce stores by scaling consistently with Facebook ads. He is one of the best to learn from.

Rank in the Maps

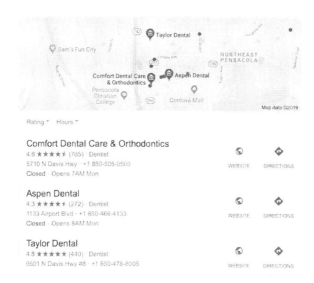

This is what it's all about, the so-called "Snack Pak" = the top 3 businesses that Google shows in the maps.

They obviously get the most traffic as users naturally click on map results first, and it's quite easy to get there as long as you stay away from busy cities and other competitive areas.

Even as a complete SEO newbie, you can rank a client in those top spots within a few weeks or less - if - you focus on smaller towns and regions with no competition.

These are the steps in a nutshell:

1) You first get them listed in *Google My Business* - otherwise, they can't show in the maps.

2) You build profiles for the business on online directories like Yelp and link back to the map profile. *Read the SEO Beginner guide* if you don't know what a backlink is and why it matters. That's important to know anyway, regardless of what direction you take in your online journey.

Directory backlinks are also called "citations" and there are plenty of inexpensive gigs that will do the job *for* you, so it really couldn't be easier.

Here is a good Google Maps Citation Gig at a whopping $13!(*)

That's mostly what it should take in a non competitive market and niche.

From then on out, there is not much else to do, unless someone else sneaks in ahead of your client, in which case you will build some more backlinks.

In the meantime, you charge the client that ongoing monthly retainer to keep them in the top spot. $500 per month is certainly possible, especially for businesses with premium services ($5,000 per client and up).

Add the next...

For more strategies and tips, also how to find such non competitive markets, you can check out this excellent beginner course from a 7-figure SEO agency owner and founder of Legiit. A whopping $97 investment:

Superstar SEO's Maps Mastery(*)

Rank Local Business Videos

Ranking local business videos works somewhat similar.

Once again, you focus on small non competitive markets with no other professional SEOs.

How do you know?

Simple. Look at the search results - "Dentist in Pensacola" in the prior example.

Do you see a lot of other videos come up?

If not - great - zero competition - go for it!

If yes, do they have that keyword, plus location, in the title?

If yes, then it's usually a sign that other SEOs are active in the area - or in that particular niche - and while you can certainly learn to outrank them, why not start with the low hanging fruit of no competition?

Again, you don't have to live in the location and you can also go into foreign countries which are usually much easier as long as you avoid big cities.

Why is ranking a Youtube video such a powerful - and easy - marketing tool for a local business?

Because Youtube is owned by Google and will always get preferential treatment over blogs and websites. You might have noticed that Youtube videos usually show up at the top of search results. That's what you are aiming for.

With the right set up, this can often happen within 24-48 hours of posting that video in a local, non competitive market!

A well known technique is "Rank & Rent":

You upload a place holder video to Youtube and use the thumbnail as a marketing billboard - either featuring your services or a specific company that you are trying to get as a client.

Then you rank that video on page 1 in Google and contact the company - or companies - if you kept it general.

You simply show them the top spot and ask them if they would like to stay there - and most will obviously say: "YES".

Who wouldn't want a top spot in Google for their business after all...?

No selling needed. You simply show results and ask if they want to keep them.

If you are shy, you can use email - or hire a sales person on Fiverr or Upwork to make those calls.

Not rocket science.

For more in-depth training, this course (also a whopping $97) shows you how it's done in more detail:

Superstar SEO's **Local Video Mastery**(*)

Personal Concierge

A personal concierge is basically the in-person version of a Virtual Assistant - and a little more upscale than a "personal assistant".

Tasks can be any of the following or more:

- *Waiting for repair men*
- *Setting appointments*
- *Organizing*
- *Preparing a move*
- *Picking up kids from school*
- *Pet care*
- *Shopping and deliveries*
- *Travel arrangements*
- *Organizing events*
- *Online research*

You don't need specific training and can get started right away by searching offers - or listing yourself - on sites like:

Care
TaskRabbit
Citizen Shipper
Instacart

Pay can vary from $25 per hour all the way up to $100 or $150 per hour depending on your expertise, tasks and clientele.

Long term, you want to build a regular client base that pays you an annual or monthly retainer, so you have a more predictable income even when clients have less need during certain times of the year.

Virtual Organizer

You have probably heard of "professional organizers" and are aware of how sought after that skill has become, but did you know that you could also become a "Virtual Organizer (VO)" and use those same skills from the comfort of your home?

How does it work?

Clients will share digital photographs or videos of their home with you or even give you a virtual walkthrough during your first session.

You can then advise them with strategies, tools and services to improve their situation and:

- *Declutter*
- *Downsize*
- *Prepare a move*
- *Time Management*
- *Overall Productivity*
- *Spring clean*
- *Feng Shui*
- *Special needs (ADHD)*

A VO is basically a remote project manager who identifies problems, sets up a solution plan and downsizes each step to manageable tasks for the overwhelmed client.

VO services keep costs low for the client. Instead of three hours for an in-person visit, they only pay for 1 hour while also saving time.

VOs provide accountability and create ongoing plans and tasks to keep clients organized and less stressed. It is usually an ongoing course of sessions, not just one time, combined with email support and homework.

NAPO, the *National Organization for Professional Organizers*, offers plenty of support and training resources and here are some more options:

Training:

Institute for Challenging Disorganization
NAPO University
OrganizingU

Welcome Service

Anytime someone moves to a new city, there are *sooo* many things to do!

It's an exhausting task and often overwhelming.

That's where you come in:

You can offer a "Welcome Service" that helps new residents get set up and connected with all the relevant services, bureaucracy, contractors, etc.

You can offer packages to help set up:

- *Utilities*
- *Car services*
- *Health care & doctor recommendations*
- *Licenses*
- *Schools & child care*
- *Pet care*
- *Gardens & lawns*
- *Cleaning services*
- *Contractors & repairmen*
- *Interior decorators*
- *Mail forwarding*

and much more.

Beyond just organizing, you can become their go-to person for all things local offering recommendations for services, restaurants and businesses, possibly offering welcome coupons and getting referral bonuses from local businesses.

Updating a new home address everywhere and mail forwarding alone can be a highly valuable service for busy professionals. They will gladly pay a premium to have it off their hands.

Virtual Bookkeeper

It may surprise you, but you don't need a fancy degree to work as a bookkeeper (not to be confused with "Accountant" or "CPA", which is quite different). If you like juggling numbers and enjoy math, you can start with $25-30 per hour as a virtual accountant, all the way up to $60 per hour.

Required is mostly a knowledge of Quickbooks or similar programs. Do a training course, learn it in-depth and you are ready to start accepting freelance work. For liability protection - since you are handling someone else's finances - business liability insurance is advisable, so you want to research that as well.

You can either build up your own clientele and market yourself on Upwork and local sites. Or you can start as a freelancer with VA Agencies and later upgrade to these higher tier companies once you have more experience:

Belay
Bookminders
ClickAccounts
AccountingDepartment

ClickNWork

For an introduction on how it all works and what you need to consider, you can watch this free class:

Bookkeeper Business Launch - Free Class(*):
"Work from Home & Earn $60+/hr by Starting Your Own "Virtual" Bookkeeping Business..."

Notary Public

Becoming a notary public is surprisingly easy. In most states, you don't even need to attend training *(though it's obviously advisable)* or pass a test! It's a little disturbing actually when I think about it. Given how important the job is, you would think there would be at least a minimal set of competency requirements, but in most states there isn't!

You have to be at least 18 years, be a legal resident of the state you want to work in, speak and write English fluently and have no criminal record (though there are some exceptions).

Beyond that, you can check your state's requirements on the **National Notary Association's website**.

After you apply, you need to get finger printed, undergo a state background check and get a bond at a bonding agency, so you are covered, in case you make a mistake.

Then you wait a few weeks to receive your notary commission in the mail. Once it arrives, you take the oath of office and get your signature registered in your county to protect against forgeries.

Next, you get your notary stamp and a journal to keep track of all transactions and clients - and you are good to go.

What exactly does a notary do?

A notary oversees the signing of important documents to:

• Prevent fraud
• Check IDs
• Make sure no one is under pressure or duress to sign
• Ensure all parties understand the terms of the document.

As for fees, check what other notaries in your area charge as it obviously varies quite a bit depending on where you live and who your clients are.

$100K/Year Collecting Trash!

I know, doesn't sound very appealing, but can be a surprisingly lucrative venture that you can mostly outsource once you have it up and running.

If you don't believe me, **check out this guy, who makes 6 Figures every year(*)** from what he calls "just taking a walk each night".

How does it work?

You find local companies, especially those in Real Estate Property Management, and offer your services. You can charge $30-50 per hour and eventually outsource the work to a team of cleaners to scale your business.

Can even turn into mostly passive income that way...

Rent Out Your Stuff

There is a whole ecosystem of online P2P renting platforms that allow you to monetize what's sitting around your closets - including items you only use on rare occasions.

With long term rentals this can even turn into passive income.

Another side benefit touted by many platforms is that renting, rather than buying, protects the environment in our consumer-heavy throw-away society.

Always be sure to read the fine print about fees, commissions and how damages are handled should they occur.

Here is a list of platforms covering different areas:

GENERAL STORES
SnapGoods
Fainin
Zilok
Loanables
RentNotBu

CARS
GetAround(*)
TravelCar

RVs
Outdoorsy
RVShare

SAILBOATS & MOTOR YACHTS
Sailo

BABY GEAR
BabyQuip
Babies Getaway
GoBaby
Traveling Baby

CAMERAS & LENSES
KitSplit

DESIGNER CLOTHES & ACCESSORIES
StyleLend
Rent My Wardrobe
DesignerShare
TheVolte
Dressed

Flip for Profit

Flea Market Flipping

Flea market flipping can be a fun and potentially lucrative past-time-turned-business.

You either find items on nearby flea markets, auctions and thrift stores or browse and app called **OfferUp** for available deals that you can flip on one of the following platforms:

ONLINE
eBay
LetGo
Ruby Lane *(Vintage)*
TIAS *(Antiques)*
Bonanza
Newegg
uBid
Listia
iOffer
eCrater
eBid

LOCAL
VarageSale
NextDoor *(Neighborhood Board)*
Facebook Marketplace
Craigslist
Oodle

How do you know a good bargain when you see one?

Experience over time, obviously, but you can also simply check on Amazon or eBay what the item is currently selling for and then strike when you see a special bargain.

FleaMarketFlipper is a blog with lots of tips and strategies, should you want to explore this option further. They also offer a training program, called:

Flipper University(*)

STAY SAFE:
*This should be obvious... but when selling in-person, never give strangers your address, but meet in well-lit public places, like a coffee shop or a Walmart parking lot. In addition, several police departments have designated trading places that are always available and have 24/7 surveillance. See a list here - "**SafeTrade**".*

Flip Used Clothes

Here is a large list of market places where you can flip clothes from thrift shops, Goodwill (or your own closet):

Poshmark
Depop
Swap
Crossroads
ASOS *(your own boutique)*
Thredup
Recycle your Fashions
Grailed
Couture
Tradesy

DESIGNER HANDBAGS & ACCESSORIES
Bag, Borrow or Steal
Fashionphile
Tradesy

WEDDING DRESSES
(also flower girl, bridesmaids and engagement rings):
Nearly Newlywed
Preowned Wedding Dresses
Still White
Sell My Wedding Dress

OLD JEWELRY
Out of your Life

Flip Used Electronics

Decluttr
Gazelle

- Video games, DVDs, CDs
- Cell phones, tablets and consoles
- Smart watches & laptops

Both sites will give you an instant cash quote and send you a pre-paid label if you accept. With Gazelle you can also drop off at a local **EcoATM kiosk** for immediate cash, though payout is usually lower.

Gameflip

A well known market place for gamers. Also, gift cards, rare movies and in-game items. Plus, gamers and designers can sell their services.

MORE PLATFORMS:
ExchangeMyPhone
SellCell

uSell
Green Buyback
Swappa
NextWorth
GameStop
YouRenew
SecondSpin
SellDVDsOnline

Amazon TradeIn *(for Gift Card only - no cash payout)*

Flip Used Books

Used Books can be traded in via the following platforms:

BookScouter
Bookfinder
Powell's
Cash4Books
Amazon TradeIn *(Gift Card only)*

You enter the ISBN codes, get a quote and then send in your books using a prepaid label. Payment is usually via Paypal.

Flip New Items

In its simplest form, you scout discount stores or major retailers for clearance sales, buy in bulk and then flip on eBay or Amazon.

"Retail Arbitrage" is a more professional version of this and works as follows:

Using the **Amazon Seller App,** you can scan bar codes of eligible items at the store, see what they sell for on Amazon, incl. all applicable fees, and then see your potential profit margin.

You need to first set up an Amazon Seller account (use the individual, free version) and once approved, you can start using the app in stores.

When you find suitable items to flip, the app creates a shipping label to an Amazon fulfillment center and you can simply drop the boxes at the next UPS center.

Once your products arrives at the center, they are ready to be sold and Amazon will guide you through each step.

This is called "Amazon FBA" (= "fulfilled by Amazon"), meaning you ship to Amazon warehouses and they take care of shipping to and communicating with customers.

All pretty straight forward and done successfully every day by thousands of people around the country - some generating 6 and 7 figure incomes.

Obviously, this will be more difficult in crowded, bigger cities as there will more competition, but I know quite a few people who started their ecom journey with Retail Arbitrage, before switching to more passive options like drop shipping, wholesaling, etc.

If you prefer some more in-depth training before getting started, you can take a look at **this course**.

PART 2
Your Passions & Interests

In the 2nd part, we'll look at even more home-based jobs and business ideas, but this time grouped by specific interests, incl. your passions and hobbies.

First, I'll cover several strategies that can be applied to any interest, so I don't keep repeating them in every chapter:

eCom Store

Any hobby or special interest will usually have a wildly passionate following that can be monetized. Creating a Shopify store with trending items and using dropshipping for fulfillment, can be one of the most lucrative ways to monetize any passion or hobby.

The more niched down the better usually, as people love specialty stores and discovering well curated items they wouldn't see at their local Walmart.
An eCom store can also easily be integrated with any other business model you are running and be largely automated with the help of VA's long term.

The key success factors for any eCom store are:

- Picking winning products
- An effective way to drive traffic to your store (aka, "Marketing")
- Building a loyal customer base of *repeat* buyers that you can keep marketing to => mailing list

Not rocket science, but you want to learn from successful sellers and not reinvent the wheel, getting nowhere.

Here is a free training by 8-figure seller Kevin David to show you how it all works:

FREE SHOPIFY BEGINNER TRAINING(*):

"The *Little Known* Shopify System I Use to Repeatably Find Viral Products on *Complete* Autopilot! *...Without ANY eCommerce experience, technical skill, or a huge upfront investment!*"

Blog or Youtube Channel

Content platforms are another logical monetization option. You could also add podcasting here though it won't apply as much to the more visual niches.

How do you monetize content platforms?

With a combination of the following:

- **Affiliate Marketing** - you recommend products and services and get paid a referral fee if someone follows your well researched suggestions and signs up. One of the most important monetization options online that any entrepreneur will and should use.

- **Information Products** - another big one: ebooks and especially online courses. More on that in the next chapter

- **Sponsorships**

- **Ads**

- **Store**

For this to work, you need to build an active, engaged following. Regular visitors to your blog or channel who love your content and trust your recommendations.

How-to's, tutorials, reviews and tips are the most important type of content here.

To learn effective growth and marketing strategies for each, you can check out these courses by some of the top performers in each field:

BLOGGING
Learn how these 2 bloggers generate $100K per month(!) from their 2 Blogs(*)

YOUTUBE
Jeven Dovey is a professional film maker and runs a Youtube channel with a 6-figure following(*)

PODCASTING
Learn from John Lee Dumas of "Entrepreneur on Fire", one of the most successful business podcasts on the planet(*)

Online Courses

Robert G. Allen of *"Nothing Down"* famously said: "I made millions with real estate, but I made *hundreds* of millions teaching it."

You can create an online course on any topic under the sun and find a hungry audience, so this applies to pretty much any skill or interest you might have.

First, you need to build an engaged following though, so you'll have someone to sell *to*.

Online courses are usually priced in the $97 to $997 range. Some even higher. Selling a high ticket item to a complete stranger who has never heard of you, is very difficult unless you are a very experienced marketer.

However, an audience that knows you, loves your content and trusts your recommendations, will love to learn more in-depth tips and strategies from you - even at a premium price.

You can then build out "sales funnels" that allow you to mostly automate the process and turn it mostly into passive income.

Another great way to build a following - actually, by far, the fastest way, is **SELF-PUBLISHING BOOKS** on Amazon!

Literally within a few weeks - as soon as you successfully publish your first book. It is also one of the fastest ways to start monetizing your passions, hobbies or interests.

Described in more detail in
HOME-BASED BUSINESS IDEAS

Be sure to download your FREE copy of the Top Selling Publishing Guide here:

BestsellerPublishing.net

YOU = Influencer

If you want to grow an influencer platform around your interest, this book will show you the 7 phases to building online influence around any topic you choose.

It's not luck whether you can reach people and build a successful brand around your passions and interests. There are clear, repeatable steps that you can take, that will get you there. You just have to:

1) *Know them*, and then...
2) *Apply them*

This book will show you exactly how:

InfluencerFastTrack.net

Live Training

Beyond books and online courses, you can, of course, also teach live - one-on-one or group classes. Either locally in your home and community or virtually through these platforms:

PrestoExperts
TakeLessons
BrainMass
Clarity
Maven
Ether

❀ ❀ ❀ ❀ ❀ ❀ ❀ ❀ ❀ ❀ ❀ ❀ ❀

Now, let's dive into some fun interests and hobbies that are well suited to build a home-based business around.

I'll start with two of my favorite things - pets and travel... :)

PETS

Dog Trainer

Love doggies, but have no formal dog training experience?

No problem, because there is **Doggy Dan**!

"Doggy Dan" is one of the top dog trainers in the world and created an excellent online course where he shares his unique - and very successful - approach to dog training.

It's a bit of a paradigm shift, but very loving, and makes a lot of sense when you see him in action. All training videos were shot in beautiful New Zealand and his own dogs often assist in the training. It's wonderful to watch - even just as a dog owner.

You can test it out for just $1 for 3 days and after that it's only $37 a month (you can cancel at any time).

Going through the entire course, incl. an extensive chapter on puppy training, will give you plenty to work with. His methods are simple and easy to repeat.

He also has a trainer certification course. It's a bit more pricey and only opens once or twice a year, but you can add it down the road.

In the meantime, you can check out his main course here:

Doggy Dan $1 Trial(*)

Dog Walker

The following three platforms make it easy to get started as a dog walker and work with a flexible schedule:

Rover
Wag!
Swifto *(NYC)*

You first have to pass through a vetting process, including a criminal background check, and prove solid dog experience.

Once accepted, you can create a profile and start taking jobs.

Wag has been called "the Uber for dogs", because the app uses a similar algorithm to pair currently available dog walkers with owners in the same neighborhood. Otherwise, all three apps work very similar.

Owners can follow along on a map where doggies walked and did their business...:) - and will receive a few furry pictures.

Payments are handled via the apps and vary depending on location. With a 97% 5-Star rating and availability in most US cities, Rover and Wag offer two great options to start in the doggy business right now.

Housesitting & Pet Boarding

House sitting has been an important and beloved part of my Digital Nomad lifestyle since 2014. I've cared for lovely fur babies all over the US, South Africa, Botswana, Australia, New Zealand, Bali, Singapore, Thailand, Dubai, Vietnam, England and Spain.

It's a great way to travel and see the world while getting a much needed "furry fix" along the way.

Demand for **local sitters and private pet hotels** is also huge, especially during vacation times, and quite well paid - at least in the US ($50+ per night).

You can offer pet boarding and doggy day care at your home or pet sit at the owner's home - either during the day, over-night or for longer stays.

The best known platforms for paid sitting and boarding are:

DogVacay
(now merged with Rover)
Rover

Wag!
Petsitter
Care

You will also find so-called "house sitting" platforms. Those are more for travelers/tourists and usually work on an exchange basis: free pet sitting in return for a free stay. Great when you travel, but not what you are looking for in a "work from home" job.

Pet Photography + POD

Pet photography is a real "thing" and beyond just photos, you can integrate with a custom POD (print-on-demand) service.

Meaning, you offer to print favorite pet photos on mugs, T-Shirts, pillow cases, and much more.

Owners love it and will pay premium prices.

Fulfillment is done through print-on-demand platforms like Gearbubble, PrinTech and many others.

You just upload the photo, purchase at wholesale price and then sell it to the client.

Phone Consultant

With **6ya** you can offer services as an animal communications expert and get paid by the minute at a rate you set.

This platform also works well if you have a following on social media, Youtube, podcast or blog. This way, you can offer your followers to get their questions answers on a quick - paid - call.

Calls are accepted through a smartphone app whenever you want to be available, so your phone number remains private.

Another option is **Ether.**

TRAVEL

Since this book is about home-based opportunities, you will not find travel jobs here (as in "work while you travel"), but rather jobs or business models in the travel industry that you can do from home.

For actual travel jobs, you can check out my **TRAVEL for FREE book**.

Local Tour Guide

Becoming a part time tour guide in your local area (worldwide) has never been easier thanks to various online platforms where you can list yourself and leverage a large pre-existing audience and marketing process.

The following sites allow you to create a profile and also handle payments for you securely through the platform in your local currency:

Vayable
Rent-A-Guide
Tours by Locals
Rent a Local Friend
Shiroube *(unusual requests)*
Advlo *(Adventure)*
AirBnB Experiences *(formerly Trip4Real)*
RentAFriend

In addition, you can, of course, network with local hotels to be recommended as a tour guide.

Remote Customer Support

Many of the major travel outfits hire remote agents for sales, customer support and vacation planning. Unlike most work-from-home jobs, which work on a freelance/independent contractor basis, travel companies often hire "employees" with all the usual benefits and paid vacation time. In addition, you get discounts on their cruises, hotels, etc.

Pay is usually a mix of hourly rate, plus bonuses or commissions and most require at least 1 year of customer service or sales experience. Don't let that stop you from applying though. If they need someone - especially during peak seasonal times - they might give you a chance if you present yourself well.

In the next chapters, you will find a list of companies that frequently hire remote workers with a link to their job boards. Quite often they also outsource to **FlexJobs**, **Glassdoor** and **Indeed,** so check those boards as well and also contact the company directly, if there is one you really want to work with.

Search "work from home", "remote" "virtual" to find relevant offers and check back frequently.

One major player in this industry with a wide variety of remote job offers and great perks is *(incl. lending you a computer and deeply discounted familiarization trips to their many travel offerings)* is:

World Travel Holdings

Remote Cruise Line Jobs

Cruises are one of the rare areas in the travel industry where people still frequently work with a travel agent - and it's highly recommended since it's impossible for an outsider to understand all the different specialties, bonuses and hidden costs among the multitude of cruise lines.

In addition, cruises are usually quite expensive, so commissions can easily be in the hundreds per sale.

Carnival Cruise Line
Holland America
Norwegian Cruise Line
Princess Cruise
Cruise.com

Franchise Opportunities:

Cruise Planners
Cruises.com

Remote Hotel Jobs
Hilton

Hyatt

Marriott

Omni

Wyndham

Airlines
Alaska Air

American Airlines

Delta

JetBlue

Southwest

Virgin Atlantic

Car Rental
Hertz

Enterprise

Business Travel Consultant
American Express

Adelman

BCD Travel

Carlson Wagonlit Travel

Theme Parks & Resorts
Disney

Exchange Student Coordinator

Local coordinators (LC) are tasked with finding families in their local community who are interested in hosting a foreign exchange student by visiting schools, churches, youth centers, etc.

They also serve as the local point of contact for exchange students during their stay.

In most cases, you will be paid a stipend for each successful placement (in some cases, up to $1,000), plus, additional perks and travel savings.

You need to be at least 25 years old and pass a criminal background check. Here are several outfits where you can apply:

American Institute for Foreign Study
Greenhart Exchange
CIEE
Aspect Foundation
Education First
STS Foundation
ICES
ERDT

Travel Blogger/Vlogger

Travel blogging is usually not considered "work from home" as travel bloggers are usually on the road a lot or are even full time nomads and location independent.

However, you can also become the top travel expert for your region or state and as such most certainly start a travel blog from home.

Growing a blog following is not an easy task and will take some time, but focusing on one specific region will make it a lot easier!

For starters, ranking locally in Google is much easier than world wide and building a following on Instagram - the must-have platform from travel bloggers - will also be a lot easier.

Once again, the fast track to success is focusing on one specific sub niche within travel. That could be:

- *Adventure*
- *Families with Children*
- *Seniors*

- *Hiking*
- *Bicycling*
- *RVs*
- *Camping*
- *Food & Beverages*
- *Music & Art Scen*
- *Road trips*

and many more. Pick something you are personally passionate about and already know a lot and then become the absolute go-to expert with lots of tips and review posts on your site.

How much you need to niche down depends, of course, on how competitive your region is. New York City will need super specific niching compared to the state of Wyoming, which has a lot to offer, but probably a lot less competition if you exclude Yellowstone.

You could also become a top expert for horse treks if you love riding. Listing all available options in your state with your personal feedback, just as an example.

Write a lot of reviews on travel outfits, tours, restaurants, etc. In most cases, you will get free access - one of the nice perks of being a travel blogger

- and they often have affiliate programs that allow you to earn a referral fee.

Affiliate marketing is one of the top income sources for bloggers and would also include your "Resources" page that every blog should have..

Another fast track to building a blog following is a bestselling Kindle book on your blog topic. Travel is not the biggest niche on Amazon, but IF you set it up right, it can be a continuous stream of new subscribers - an income. My **Quick Guide on Bali** for example has earned me about $20,000 so far - and took only 1 week to write! It also frequently outranked *Lonely Planet* and even *"Eat, Pray, Love"*.

Kindle books are short - even 10K words are fine - and you can easily combine a number of relevant blog posts into a book. The title of "Bestselling Author" will give you a lot more credibility and it's not that hard to achieve if you know how (ethically and by Amazon's TOS, of course - no scam tactics!).

If you want to learn first-hand from one of the most successful travel bloggers in the world, then check out Nomadic Matt's course:

Nomadic Matt' Travel Blogging Course(*)

Matt also partnered with several other legends of the travel influencer scene to help you become a successful:

Travel Vlogger(*) *(Hey Nadine)*
Travel Writer(*) *(David Farley)*
Travel Photographer(*) *(Laurence Norah)*

...if that's more up your alley.

Travel Writer

The following publications pay for guest articles:

Go Nomad
International Living
Ireland Before You Die
Outpost Magazine
Travelicious
Wanderful
International Living

Instagram Travel

Instagram is the must-have social media platform for travel professionals.

You can either build a following in tandem with a blog or vlog - or just focus on Instagram alone.

Travel outfits will frequently pay for sponsored posts or shoutouts on travel pages with a large, active following or invite you to free trips and tours, incl. press tours (fully paid).

Instagram has become a lot more difficult to grow on thanks to a number of recent algorithm changes and you need to learn from someone who is always up to date on what is currently working.

Josue Pena has grown pages for Gary V, Alex Becker and Kevin David and teaches one of the best Instagram courses (also for the agency option, mentioned in a prior chapter).

You can check out a Free Training Video here:

"The Weird System That Gets Me 50K Followers A Month AND A $200K Dollar Paycheck...

...without using bots, or fake followers AND how you can easily knock if off in less than 1 Day"

ARTS & CRAFTS

Calligraphy

If you always had a knack for beautiful, stylish handwriting, a calligraphy side hustle could be for you. Rates are pretty good. Just addressing envelopes can bring in $2-$5 per piece.

To learn the ropes, you want to get a starter kit from a well-known calligrapher (Google "Top 10...." "Best..." etc.) and book an intro class in your area, so you can learn the fundamentals.

From there, continue to learn and improve with online courses or even Youtube videos - and *practice.* A lot! Even experienced pros keep practicing and improving their skills. Keeping that muscle memory alive.

As for marketing, referrals are usually the fastest way to get started. Baby showers, engagements and weddings, store openings, school graduations - just put the word out to your local community and network with related professionals (event and wedding planners, pastry chefs, caterers, hotels, etc.).

Etsy is another place where you can promote your calligraphy business - and also use it to process payments.

Otherwise, social media, in particular the visual ones like Instagram and Pinterest. You can even start a Youtube channel with tutorials and tips.

Sell your Crafts

If you are a "crafty" one... :) you'll find plenty of online options to monetize those skills. You can obviously sell locally to shops and fairs. Beyond that, the internet has opened up a whole new dimension of sales platforms to reach thousands and potentially millions of customers.

Below is a list of currently available platforms. Obviously, those change from time to time as some shut down and new ones come along, but it will give you plenty of options to get started:

Aftcra
Zibbet
Artfire
iCraft
Shopvida
Novica
Storfenvy
BigCartel

UK
Folksy

Poster My Wall

Create posters for parties, promotions, bands, graduations, bake sales and more.

Not a market place, but the premier platform to build your own store and shopping website:

Shopify(*)

To showcase and market your crafts, Pinterest is an ideal platform and comes with several additional benefits:

- Pinterest is the only social media platform where people come to buy or get buying ideas and inspirations.

- It is the ideal marketing platform for anything ecom and most Etsy sellers use Pinterest actively to drive traffic to their stores.

- Google "loves" Pinterest and automatically ranks popular pins and boards on page 1, driving additional free traffic to your store.

- Pins can remain "evergreen" hits. Unlike other social media platforms where posts are only relevant for a day or so, viral pins can stay at the top of search results for a long time, bringing you evergreen traffic => passive income.

These two bloggers get almost all their traffic from Pinterest and have grown their two blogs to $100K per month in earnings, just from Pinterest traffic (yes, per MONTH!).

They have a wonderful course and active Facebook group where you can learn their strategies:

Pinterest Traffic Avalanche(*)

Drawings

Very similar to the prior chapter. Here are 10 online market places where you can sell your designs. Several are "POD" or print-on-demand outlets that allow you to place your designs on T-Shirts, mugs, posters, phone cases, canvas and much more:

Creative Market
Designs by Humans
Poster My Wall
Design Cuts
ArtWeb
ArtistShops
Society 6
BigCartel
Etsy

FONTS
My Fonts

More stringent Application Process:
This is a Limited Edition
Imprnt
Not on the High Street

WRITING

Writing is obviously a vast field with many different sub categories. In this book, we'll focus on some of the best known options, but you could also focus on copywriting, grant writing, technical writing, ghost writing and many, many more.

If you love writing, but have struggled so far to turn it into a well-paid profession, you might want to check out this course from a very successful freelance writer:

30 Days of Less to Freelance Writing Success(*)

and this resource to give you some ideas:

200+ Writing Niches(*)

Now, let's check out some of the heavy weights among writing gigs:

Write for Blogs & Magazines

Paid writing gigs will usually not accept newbie writers, but prefer to see a track record and how your writing has been received by readers in the past.

However, many blogs will accept guest posts. They are mostly unpaid, but usually allow a bio and links to your website, social media, etc., so you at least get free traffic. Plus, you are building your portfolio and can later transition to paid work.

You want to offer a "lead magnet" in your bio, meaning a free cheatsheet, report, checklist, training video, or similar that readers can access in return for providing their email address. That way, guest blogging can also turn into an effective way to grow your following and mailing list.

Before you pitch to a blog owner, be sure to carefully read their requirements and how they want you to submit - then follow it to the letter. Include a few samples of your work - or published posts if you have - and follow up after a week or so.

If you want to fast track the process and also get access to editor contacts of over 100 top blogs and magazines, you definitely want to check out Jon Morrow's guest blogging training. He is one of the most successful bloggers - and guest bloggers - of our time and was paid and average of $7,000 per article(!) when he was still guesting.

Now he is mostly focused on his own 8 figure blog - *Smartblogger* - all that while being paralyzed from the neck down! A very inspiring story and the one course that opened all doors for me when I first started.

You can check it out here:
**How to get the Attention of Editors at
Top Blogs and Online Magazines(*)**

If you feel ready for paid gigs, you can start submitting to the companies below. They all work with freelance writers:

COMPANIES HIRING WRITERS:

**Dotdash
Online Writing Jobs
BKA Content
Wise Bread**

MetroParent

Cactus

EditFast

LoveToKnow

iWriter

ZenContent

Funds for Writers

Bustle

TIPS & SHORT STORIES

Chicken Soup for the Soul

Country Magazine

Cuisine at Home

Eating Well

KnowledgeNut

Take a Break

The Story People

Family Handyman

Finescale Modeler

That's Life UK

Knitty

SheMedia

International Living

Doctor of Credit

FREELANCE WRITER PLATFORMS:

Verblio
Freelancer
Guru
iFreelance
Online Writing Jobs
Outsourcely
People Per Hour
Upwork
Textbroker
Toptal

FREELANCE WRITER JOB BOARDS:>

BloggingPro
Direct Response Jobs
FlexJobs
Freelance Writing
Freelance Writing Jobs
Problogger

POETRY

Grain Magazine
Sojourners

The Sun Magazine

GREETING CARDS

Blue Mountain
Comstock

Here is a massive list of 100 websites and magazines that pay you to write and how much they pay!

100 Websites that Pay You to Write

Publish Bestsellers!

The absolute fastest way to monetize your writing
and grow a worldwide following:

Described in the Intro of Part 2

Grab your FREE Copy for the
Top Selling Publishing Guide at:

BestsellerPublishing.net

Blogger

Also described in the Intro of PART 2

StartACoolBlog.net

Corporate Writer

Corporate freelance writing is one of the overlooked gems in the writing profession - and can be extremely lucrative.

You are not competing with every writer on the planet. Instead, corporate writers are a much smaller, more exclusive group.

My publishing student Jeanette Jureyea turned this gig into a 7 Figure empire in just a few years and wrote this insightful guide to help others break into this highly lucrative field:

#1 Bestselling Book:
"Corporate Freelance Writing made Easy:
How I Earned Over $1 Million in Seven Years without
Guerrilla Marketing"

Write Resumes & Cover Letters

Writing resumes and cover letters is one of the least favorite jobs for most people.

That means, plenty of opportunities for you to earn some extra cash!

To put this into perspective: According to Fiverr, one of their top sellers, Charmaine Pocek, initially offered a gig writing cover letters and resumes for just $5 a pop. Within a few years, she was charging up to $800 for her services, eventually crossing $2 million in sales - just on Fiverr!

Quite the potential...

If you are not an expert - and who is... - there are plenty of guides online on how to best write a professional resume and cover letter. Including best styles and designs.

American Writers & Artists Inc. offers an **online course on Pro Resume Writing**.

To promote your services you can start within your immediate network. Almost everyone needs a resume at one point or another and you can build up a portfolio and testimonials. You can also list yourself on the typical freelancer platforms - Upwork, Fiverr, etc., or look for resume jobs on these boards:

JOB BOARDS for RESUME WRITERS:

ResumeEdge
RiseSmart
Boardroom Resumes
FlexJobs
Talent Inc.
Upwork

Once you have a steady flow of clients, you can start outsourcing some of the work to other freelancers while you focus on marketing and getting more clients. That's called "arbitraging" and a common practice in the freelance world.

PHOTO & VIDEO

I will not cover the obvious choices like wedding and portrait photography, but rather focus you on some lesser known options that you can offer even if you are not a professional photographer:

Specialty Photo/Videography

Becoming an expert in one specific niche is one of the main success factors in almost any business. Ever more so in the overcrowded photography scene.

Even without years of experience, you can gain traction and happy customers if you become the go-to person in your area for say:

- Food Photography *(well paid and a much needed specialty)*
- Pet Portraits *(see also the next chapter on custom merch)*
- Babies *(no words needed)*
- Houses for sale or AirBnB listings
- eComm items and Crafts
- Gardens

and many more.

Pick a niche that excites you, that you spend much time on anyway. You probably already know a lot of people in that scene, so getting clients and word-of-mouth promotion will be all the easier. People will trust you and your instincts, because you are "one of them" and understand what's important, much more so than an outside professional photographer.

Make sense?

As for skills:

The internet has made it so much easier to improve your photo and video chops without going through months and years of trial and error or expensive schools.

Here is Shutterstock's list of 11 Youtube Channels every Photographer should follow.

And these are some excellent channels on videography:

Peter McKinnon
Think Media
Potato Jet
Cinecom
Jeven Dovey

Beyond that, you can find plenty of inexpensive tutorials on Skillshare and Udemy, also for Photoshop, Lightroom and video editing software.

Everything can be learned and all the info you need has become easily available via the internet.

Pair that with something you are passionate about and have unique insights in, and you can turn this into a well-run - enjoyable - business.

Custom Mugs 'n Stuff

When taking photos of babies, pets, anniversaries and other events that are important and dear to your customers, you can offer to print their favorite pics on mugs, T-shirts, phone cases, pillows, tote bags and even jewelry.

Several print-on-demand platforms offer the option of custom orders, meaning you can upload a picture during checkout and choose the item the customer wants it placed on (mugs, T-shirts, etc.).

You purchase at wholesale prices and sell to the customer at a markup.

This is a very popular option that people happily pay a premium price for - and is very easy to add from your end.

Microstock

Microstock sites for both photo and video footage can provide another possible income stream, and passive income at that.

The first blueprint in my *passive income book* goes into more detail.

Here is the short version:

Stock footage are short video clips (or photos) of usually just a few seconds, featuring every day scenes.

They are used as fillers in larger productions:

- *Commercials or commercial videos for companies*
- *TV Shows (remember that intro from "House of Cards"?)*
- *Explainer videos*
- *YouTube*

and many more. Same with photos.

To monetize, you need to upload your footage to the major stock sites where customers can find and download them.

If your footage is popular, this can happen over and over again - creating a consistent, passive income stream that didn't take a lot of time to create.

It's quite tedious initially to upload everything one by one and to various different stock platforms, but for video, there is now fortunately a service called **Blackbox** that takes care of all that.

You only have to upload each photo and video once, including title and tags, and the platform distributes to all the major sites. You can even partner with someone on Blackbox to do the uploading for you for a profit share.

Video stock is a *lot* more lucrative than photos - from $20 to $200 per video download (especially in 4K), so you want to focus on mostly video from the start.

You don't need to be a professional film maker. Your smart phone is perfectly fine in the beginning - many even have 4K now. It's much more important that you get an eye for what sells. What motives, themes, etc.

You also need to learn about lighting and some basic editing. Possibly color grading.

Take a few classes (Youtube, Skillshare, etc.) and then practice a lot. Keep an eye on the top selling videos and try to emulate their style (don't copy obviously...).

To speed up the learning curve , I recommend this course by professional film maker and 6-figure Youtuber Jeven Dovey. He makes a full-time income from stock footage alone ($6,000/month), in addition to his other ventures, and he can help you avoid a lot of the pitfalls and beginner mistakes that keep most stock artists from ever making any significant money.

You get a 7-day free trial, so no risk at all:

How To Make Money Selling Stock Footage(*)

Here are some of the typical stock sites:

Shutterstock
Adobe Stock
Fotolia
iStock
BigStock

Dreamstime
SnapWire

This app allows you to upload and sell directly from your smartphone:

Foap

Video Intros & Outros

A fun side gig that you can offer on **Fiverr** or **Legiit** and quite easy to do. You don't need to be an editing or special effects ninja. Instead, you can simply buy a cool intro template on places like **Envato Elements,** a monthly subscription that gives you unlimited downloads and then insert photos, videos and text that the customer provided you. Add some cool music - done!

You can get royalty free, high quality music on **Musicbed(*)** and **Epidemic Sound,** the two main places Youtubers use for their channels - or in many cases, the customer will have a song in mind (just make sure it's properly licensed!).

Once you get the hang of it, you can churn these out very quickly - offer several different templates to choose from and then simply enter the info. Or train a VA to do it.

Review Photos & Videos

Stock sites like Shutterstock occasionally hire remote "Image Reviewers" (or "Video Reviewers") to moderate the thousands of new photo and video submissions they receive every week.

The reviewer evaluates:

• Overall quality
• Technical execution
• Commercial suitability
• Adherence to company standards
• Check trademark and copyright requirements

Once images are accepted, the reviewer will also apply metadata (title, tags, etc.), select keywords to drive search engine traffic and provide honest, concise feedback to the contributor.

This gig requires a thorough background in photography or videography and the ability to handle fast paced, high volume work loads with detail and precision. Image reviewer positions are usually posted on job boards like FlexJobs or Indeed or on the stock sites themselves.

FASHION

Virtual Stylist

Virtual stylists assist people who struggle to find the right outfits and/or want to develop a look that really suits them. You consult on style and find the best clothing items for clients - either locally as a personal shopper or via online platforms like **StitchFix** and **Operator**.

On **StitchFix**, customers first fill out a style profile. Then a "Personal Stylist" gets to work and handpicks pieces that fit their tastes, needs and budget and ships them to the customer (on a monthly subscription). Each box contains a curated selection of clothing, shoes and accessories for the customer to try. They can keep what they like and return the rest in a prepaid envelope. The stylist earns a commission on any item the customer buys.

With **Operator**, customers get online shopping help from an expert whenever they want to buy. Not only for fashion, but also Home Goods and Tech if you have expertise in those areas.

On Operator, stylists can also create curated collections that are featured on the app, providing an additional way to attract new clients who love your style and want to work with you. Plus, passive income from any purchases resulting directly from the collection.

To apply, you need to prove solid experience in the fashion industry. Stylists for either platform are thoroughly vetted to ensure customers get a great experience. If you love fashion (and shopping...:), this can be a fun freelance gig, also long term.

Here are several more companies for Virtual Stylists:

FASHION
Trunk Club
Bombfell
Stella & Dot *(also Jewelry)*

JEWELRY & ACCESSORIES
Emmy & Cloe
Rockbox
Hangsquad
Your Bijoux Box

Personal Shopper (local)

If you want to build your own local Personal Shopper business, you can list yourself on sites like:

Thumbtack
Style Careers
Fashion Jobs

or check with major department stores in your area (Bloomingdales has as program for example).

This article will give you a good introduction and valuable tips on how to get started:

"Things I wish I knew before becoming a Personal Shopper"

Fashion Direct Sales

If you are not a fashion professional, but would love to sell clothes, beauty products or jewelry, a direct sales company might be an option.

You have probably heard of Avon and there are many other companies like it. Most function in an MLM (Multilevel or "Network" Marketing) structure, meaning you can earn money both from your own sales, but also a percentage from sales of "associates" in your network (who you recruited).

Direct Sales companies are not necessarily the same as MLM. There is overlap with some, but many do not use an MLM structure and can be a valid business opportunity.

In some cases, they might pair you as a "personal stylist" with customers that visit their website, similar to the "Virtual Stylist" option described before.

Some people have amazing success with Direct Sales companies and absolutely love this business opportunity. Others have been burned, so use common sense and don't invest much money initially. This is crucial as you will often be pressured to buy a lot of start up inventory (run the other way if that happens!) - and be careful with overly sensational sales pitches.

Here is a list of 20 Direct Sales companies in the fashion and beauty arena.

Flip Clothes OnlineOnline

Described in the "FLIP FOR PROFIT" CHAPTER - Click HERE

COOKING

Micro Restaurant

If you live in a tourist-rich area and love to cook, you can monetize that skill by offering so-called "food experiences".

You could turn your home into a "micro restaurant" and host travelers from around the world who love meeting locals and learn about different cuisines.

Very popular are also cooking classes and food tours to your favorite local hotspots. The following apps make it easy to connect - and get paid for your passion - while meeting interesting people and making new friends:

EatWith
Eat At A Locals
EatAway
BonAppetour
CookApp
CoLunching
MealSharing
ChefsFeedExperiences

OFFER COOKING CLASSES:
Cookly

On-Demand Cooking

Similarly, you can get bookings for local dinner parties and events, and offer cooking classes on these sites. Most accept amateur gourmet chefs:

BookACook
HireAChef
TableAtHome
TakeAChef

Meal Delivery

Many people are too busy to cook, but would love to get good, healthy meals delivered to their door.

A friend of mine recently mentioned how he had tried to start with the ketogenic diet, but found it difficult and time consuming to get all the proper ingredients. Plus, he didn't enjoy cooking much. So he put out an ad to find a local keto expert to cook and deliver meals for him every day.

He quickly found a local lady who knew the diet well and pre-cooked a weekly supply for him that he could store in his freezer and just heat up every day. He *loved* it! - and there are many more like him...

Whether it's keto or vegan or any other trending diet, there will be plenty of people in your local area who would love to have someone just cook it for them - and pay a premium price for that luxury.

You can list yourself on:
HireAChef
Craigslist
TaskRabbit
Local Newspapers & Boards

Sell your Creations

Localvore connects local producers, restaurants and chefs with food lovers who want to support the local foodie scene.

If you grow organic veggies, bake delicious bread or make gourmet jams, you can connect with customers through this platform.

To reach a larger customer base beyond your local region, you can sell online at:

Goldbelly
Etsy

Sell Recipes & Tips

Selling your recipes and cooking tips can be a fun extra income source and help spread your name - especially, if you run a food blog, Youtube channel or Instagram page.

Professional looking photos are key here. Food photography is a well paid specialty and you need to either learn it yourself or hire a food photographer. Not just for recipes, but also for any other food related content you create and items or services you sell.

Another option is to hire a recipe writer on Fiverr or Upwork. Recipe writing is an art and requires a lot of specific detail, but there are plenty of freelancers to choose from and many offer food photography as part of the gig - in some cases, even video.

Numerous food blogs and magazines accept submissions for guest posts - either recipes or tips - and quite a few of them are paid ($10-20 per recipe usually). Here are a few examples, but there are many more.

Recipe Yum
Cooking Light
Sunset
Cooking for Engineers

Cuisine
(Cuisine pays $100 for solving common cooking problems)

To see what a particular publication/magazine pays per article, visit this site: **Who Pays Writers**

For more tips on landing guest posts on bigger blogs and magazines, you can check out this resource by 8 figure blogger Jon Morrow. It's a course I did in the very beginning of my writing career and it has made all the difference in my writing and entrepreneurial career. Many of my students have taken it as well and are all raving. The course also includes a "Big Black Book" with direct contact info to editors of 103 top magazines and blogs, incl. Huffington Post, Lifehacker and many more.

Top Rated Guest Blogging Training(*)

You can also sell your articles in Facebook groups that connect content creators with bloggers who are interested in buying. Join as many as you can, respect the rules and offer your content. Here are two examples to get you started:

Blogger Resource Room
Pinterest Friendly Content for Bloggers

Etsy allows you to sell recipes in your shop as an add-on.

Finally, recipe contests can be fun, earn you some money and help grow your following:

RECIPE CONTESTS

Taste of Home
Contest Cook
Better Recipes

Teach Kids Healthy Cooking

Another franchise opportunity and a very rewarding one:

Giving you an opportunity to help fight child obesity and get children excited about healthy habits.

As a *Healthy Hands Cooking Instructor* you will run your own local franchise business offering healthy cooking classes to local children.

The company has partnered with Nick Jr's Butterbean Cafe as well as 100+ community partners all around the country who support the effort by providing a clean space for the classes and co-marketing to their audience.

Healthy Hands Cooking describes itself as a "cooking instructor online training program". However, it offers a lot more than just cooking classes. You are given a blueprint to start and run your own business, complete with all the necessary backend tools (website, payment processing, marketing tools, etc.) to make your new venture a success.

Ongoing training and a vibrant peer community are part of the fun.

You don't need to be an expert cook or experienced instructor. An online training course will teach you everything you need to know and you can complete it at your own pace from your computer.

In addition to cooking and nutrition instructions, you'll receive guidance on proper licensing, permits, background checks, food safety, marketing and more.

Foo∂ Blogger/Tuber/IGer

Cooking and anything related to healthy food and specific diets is one of the most lucrative fields for any content creator. Be it a blog, Youtube channel or Instagram.

Of course, it's also one of the most competitive, so just putting out a blog and hoping for the best, will do nothing.

There are specific strategies for each platform that have proven to work and can help newbies grow quickly - even with all the competition. This is something you need to learn from a pro or you will just waste a lot of time creating content that no one will ever see - and then give up in frustration.

Running a blog, channel or Instagram page is a business and it's important to be clear about that.

You are learning a new profession that comes with a learning curve and quite a bit of time investment, especially in the beginning. You are "going back to school" so to speak and you want to take it just as seriously.

With that mindset in place, you can absolutely grow a following on these platforms and start monetizing within a few months (often even sooner).

Monetization comes from selling your products (ebooks, courses, services, etc.) as well sponsorships and affiliate marketing (= you get a referral fee when recommending a product).

Once your blog, channel or IG page has an engaged following and gets a lot of consistent traffic, things get a lot easier and some of it will turn into passive income.

Here are several excellent training resources to get you started, all created by 6 and 7 figure earners with thousands of successful students and active Facebook support groups to help you along the way and network with fellow students:

BLOGGING

These bloggers turned their 2 blogs into 100K/month!

Pro Blogger Bundle(*)

The majority of their blog income comes through Pinterest traffic and they share in this course how - either as part of the bundle or by itself.

Pinterest Traffic Avalanche(*)

YOUTUBE

Jeven Dovey(*)

INSTAGRAM

Carla Biesinger(*)
Carla is specialized on food & food photography as well as landing premium consulting clients through Instagram Hint: the number of followers is not what matters...

You can start with her
FREE Insta Bootcamp(*)

HEALTH & WELLNESS

Mom Fitness Franchise

Fit4Mom provides fitness classes for Moms - with strollers!

Classes include such fun offerings as "Stroller Strides", "Fit4Baby", "Body Back" and "Mama Well"...

What Mom would not want to be a part of that fun sisterhood..?

The best part: If you love fitness and Mom-hood, you can either start as an instructor at a local franchise - or - open your own franchise with the full support of the Fit4Mom mothership behind you.

Named a **"Top Business for Moms"** by *Working Mother Magazine* and **"One of the fastest growing franchises"** by *Entrepreneur Magazine*, *Fit4Mom* is more than just a fitness workout with your toddler. More than 300 franchises all over the country create a supportive and fun community for over 1,000,000 Moms nationwide striving for a healthy lifestyle.

Find out more here (and watch a cute video):

Fit4Mom Franchise

❀❀❀❀❀❀❀❀❀

Moms on the Run is another wonderful franchise option in the Mom/Fitness arena. This one more focused on running, walking and endurance fitness.

No strollers here...:) - but also a place to foster community and help fellow Moms live a healthier life and achieve goals they never thought possible (like running their first 5K!).

More info (and another cute video) here:

Moms on the Run

Online Fitness Coach

Team Beachbody is a direct sales company that allows you to build your own coaching business - _online_!

That's right. You are not out and about teaching lessons, but your main job is to accompany customers on their journey, hold them accountable and keep them motivated.

You don't have to be in top shape yourself, but you should be actively working on your own goals and participate in the accountability challenges.

As a Team Beachbody Coach you meet with customers online to discuss their needs and design a plan to get their desired body. The company provides its own fitness routines that you help customers to implement.

You run accountability groups (Facebook) - so-called "Challenge Groups". Each day, clients check in and report their diet and whether they were able to complete the workout - and of course, also a lot of fun stuff, supporting each other and sharing tips.

"UBER" Massage

If you are a passionate massage therapist, but find fixed employee hours grinding, **Soothe** might be a good solution for you.

Soothe is an app that connects local clients with available mobile massage therapists to come to their home, office, hotel or event in as little as an hour.

Kinda like an UBER massage....

Once listed, you can set your own hours and respond to calls when you feel like it.

The website claims that earnings are 2-3 times the industry standard. For safety, they provide 24/7 phone support and GPS check in and out on all appointments.

Soothe is currently available in the US, Canada, the UK, Germany and Australia.

Get Paid to Lose Weight!

HealthyWage and **DietBet** will literally pay you for losing weight!

How does *that* work?

First, you define your weight goals and a time limit to achieve those goals.

Next, you either join an existing challenge team on the app or you create your own with a few friends. You can also ask for help in finding a team. Basically, you are placing a financial bet on your success - usually between $20 to $500 per month (depending on how long the challenge lasts).

If you don't succeed, you lose it all, but if you reach your goal, the "jackpot" is split among all successful participants who reached their target weight - sometimes $10,000 or more!

A brilliant idea to keep people motivated during their weight loss journey and have fun along the way as both apps provide a lot of interactions between participants.

Get Paid to be Active!

StepBet works exactly the same way as the weight loss challenges in the previous chapter, except now your fitness goals are being tracked.

Achievement works a little differently. This app also tracks your movements throughout the day, incl. step count and sleep logs.

It connects to your regular health apps and runs continuously in the background. The more apps you connect, the more earning opportunities you have.

Once you earn 10,000 points, you can have $10 deposited into your bank account.

Get paid for healthy actions!

Teach Kids Healthy Cooking

Described in the **COOKING CHAPTER** *(though you don't need to be an experienced cook for this one)*.

Get Paid to Stay in Bed!

This one's a bit extreme, but also *extremely* well paid:

$19,000 for staying in bed for 70 days!

No joke!

That's how much **NASA** pays participants of their *Bed Rest Study*, which helps them investigate how the human body changes as it adjusts to weightlessness in space *(somehow staying in bed for 70 days, simulates that weightless state)*.

Participants have to stay in bed for most of those 70 days, which sounds easier than it is, but at that payout certainly an interesting option.

At the time of this writing, they were searching for German speaking participants for the September 2019 study, *just so you know I'm not making this up...:)*

GARDENING

Lawn Care

Lawn care is always in demand and if you own a motorized lawn mower, you could add a side hustle (or full-time gig) on the green.

These apps can connect you with local customers - and can also get you a sense of how much demand there would be, if you decided to pursue this option:

Greenpal
Lawnly
LawnStarter
Plowz & Mowz

Host Flower Arranging Parties

How about getting paid to run flower arranging parties for women in your area!

Sound like fun?

An no, you don't need any experience in flower arranging.

Alice's Table is an online platform and community that provides women with the tools and expertise to launch their own flower arranging business. They can host floral events and workshops, arrange flowers for special occasions or hold flower arranging events at restaurants, book stores, bachelorette parties, etc.

The company was a ***winner of Shark Tank*** and scored ***endorsements from Marc Cuban and Sara Blakely***!

The website offers a backend office to members for supplies, teaching materials and an Eventbrite style event management platform, incl. ticket sales.

New members are provided with in-depth training and ongoing coaching calls. For more info and to sign up visit:

Alice's Table

Write for Horticultural Mags

The following magazines accept paid submissions from experts in gardening and farming:

Horticulture Magazine
Sunset Magazine
The American Gardener
The Maine Organic Farmer
The Canadian Organic Grower

Gardening Courses & Classes

Local gardening and horticultural classes are one option, especially for specific flowers, plants or veggies.

You can also teach through online courses on Udemy and Skillshare (=passive income) or in an online classroom on sites like **TakeLessons** or your very own Youtube Channel or blog.

KIDS

Baby Planner

Just like there are wedding planners, there are actually "Baby Planners".

If you have the experience and love kids, you can become a life saver for stressed and overwhelmed parents-to-be.

You are basically a personal consultant, and you can choose a sub niche like eco-friendly, luxury or budget, or focus on specific phases of the journey, like bed rest, birth prep, post-birth, etc.

Bed Rest Concierge is an inspiring example of a wonderful start-up that came out of seeming tragedy, but was already valued at over 3 Million Dollars, just a year after starting. Be sure to watch the video...

Bed rest is one example and as an experienced Mom, you will have plenty more ideas of what mothers and parents-to-be need most urgently - and make that your niche.

The next chapter is one such niche that even turned into a franchise opportunity:

Baby Bodyguard

"**Baby Bodyguards**" - what a cool name!

Founded by a husband and wife team from Brooklyn, and now expanding into franchises across the US, the company offers expecting and new parents the following three services:

- Baby proofing your house
- Proper Baby car seat installation
- Infant & child CPR classes

Most parents are worried about the many things that could happen once the little sunshine moves into the house and having professional support is a welcome service.

You can build your own business if you have experience and certifications, or build a franchise under the **Baby Bodyguard** brand with training, materials and clear action plans already in place.

Baby Swimming Instructor

A beautiful business opportunity and also available in other countries beyond the US.

ISR - *Infant Swimming Resource* - is training instructors in the ISR method for teaching infants to float and swim. Instructors can then build their own business in their local communities under the ISR brand.

Rather than talking about it, I invite you to watch this beautiful video. It will make you smile and tug at your heart.... :)

Teach Babies how to Swim.

Baby & Maternity Consignment Franchise

Named one of the *"TOP 10 Franchises to Buy"* by *Forbes Magazine* 3 years in a row, **Just Between Friends** offers an entry into the booming Consignment Sales Event industry, focusing specifically on children's and maternity clothes and accessories.

This is how it works:

Franchise owners provide a marketplace for families to buy and sell during at least two large consignment events each year.

- Families can get great bargains at the fraction of the price of retail
- Consignors can earn money back on gently worn baby and maternity items
- Franchise owner makes a percentage on any item sold.
- Donated, unsold items go to local charities

A quadruple win-win, in other words.

Training and ongoing support are provided and you purchase a territory that only you cover.

Buying a retail franchise is not a small matter and comes with a significant investment - though a lot less than retail franchises would normally run. Given the huge popularity of consignment sales, earning potential is significant.

For much more info and some introductory videos, click here:

Just Between Friends Franchise

Drive Kids

As described in the **Car jobs chapter** - several apps need drivers specifically for children:

Zum

HopSkipDrive
The UBER for Kids and Schools
Currently offers a promotion for new drivers:
$1,000 guaranteed the 1st month after 40 rides in 30 days
(Confirm current offers)

Teach Kids Healthy Cooking

Described in the **COOKING CHAPTER** *(though you don't need to be an experienced cook for this one).*

Kid's Party Planner

Children's parties can be another lucrative local business with parents spending up to $1,000 on birthday parties and even more on graduations, baby showers,
quinceañeras, etc.

You need to network and negotiate with local vendors, performers and venues. Be up-to-date on trends and what kids are currently into. And - *obviously* - be a great organizer.

Network in your local community with childcare centers, kindergardens, schools, etc., to connect with interested parents.

Offer a few highly discounted parties to get a foot in the door and start generating buzz as word of mouth can be your greatest marketing tool with this one.

Tutor

See more info in the TUTOR CHAPTER - both in-person and online/virtual.

Kids Day Care Care

Discussed in the HOME CHAPTER - click here

Children's Book Author

I already mentioned the joys and rewards of self-publishing.

A special sub genre are children's books and my friend and fellow bestselling author Eevi Jones is the expert on that.

You can attend her **FREE Masterclass HERE(*).**

To get an overall sense how publishing works, feel free to download this book while it's free:

BestsellerPublishing.net

VIDEO GAMES

Test Games

PlayTest Cloud is one of the rare platforms that pays decent money to game testers.

According to their website, payment is generally $9 for a 15 minute play test and survey, which is not bad, compared to the cents or reward points you usually get for these types of reviews.

No special skills required. You simply sign up, share what devices you use and go through a brief training, so you know how to perform the tests. Then - start playing!

Global Beta Test Network is a worldwide gamer community (18+). They frequently need participants for so-called "stress tests", which are used to determine stability and strength of multi-player video games and consoles. No special skills or experience required, just the necessary hardware as they will specify. Pay is by hourly rate and you sign an NDA.

Nintendo: If you live near Redmond, WA, you can also apply to be a tester *(on location)* for Nintendo. They recruit through ***Parker Services*** and ***Aerotek***.

Play Games Live

Twitch is the Youtube for game aficionados.

Gamers can live stream their sessions and interact with their audience (often in the tens or even hundreds of thousands!). You don't have to be advanced, but you need to be entertaining.

Top streamers can earn hundreds of thousands of dollars per month(!). Monetization happens through tipping, ad revenue and subscriptions.

Flip Games

Of course, you can also sell or flip games or gamer related items on **Gameflip.**

Aside from video games, they also allow you to sell gift cards, rare movies and in-game items.

Coach other Gamers

Yep - you can actually make money teaching other gamers, be it strategies and tips for specific games that you master or basic lingo for beginners.

Several platforms allow you to share your teaching gigs with the gaming community:

Gamer Sensei
Coaches are "Senseis" and teach specific games

Gameflip Gigs
Gameflip is a well known market place for video games and equipment. They recently added a "Gigs" feature for coaches and creatives (designers).

eSport Competitions

Video game competitions have turned into a billion dollar industry. Yes, that's billion with a "B".

Hundreds of millions of people tune in live for some of these events.

In 2018 the League of Legends World Championships attracted 200 million viewers - compared to 100 Million at the Super Bowl!

Esports are rivaling their "real" counterparts in audience enthusiasm and so-called MOBAs (Massive Online Battle Arenas) trump them all.

So....if you are a top gamer who can play in the big leagues, there's a lot of money to be made. Esport giants like Blizzard Entertainment, Epic Games and Riot Games pay out up to $100 million at international events, so…

If your mama told you not to play - think again…:)

MEDICAL

This chapter does not focus on medical professionals, but people who are interested in the medical field and would like to build a home-based opportunity around it.

GoodStart Mentor

Pleio GoodStart offers a home-based business opportunity as a "**GoodStart Mentor**" helping patients establish a good medication routine and providing them with ongoing support, info, resources and phone reminders.

Training is provided free of charge.

Retrieve Patient Records

ParaMeds hires remote staff to call medical facilities and request patient records. Search for "Remote Records Retrieval Specialists"

Medical Coding & Billing

Medical coders review patient records and apply proper codes for insurance billing.

May not sound like super fun, but is always in high demand and a pretty well paid gig with quite a few remote options available.

You need to get trained and certified at a facility like **Career Step** and then you are ready to apply at the following platforms - or through the regular job boards:

The Coding Network
Career Assist
AviaCode
AAPC
United Health Group
nThrive
GeBBS
Change Health Care
McKesson
eBilling Solutions

Medical Transcription

To get into medical transcription, you should be familiar with medical terminology, anatomy, physiology, etc. Most companies prefer to hire professionals who are certified though it is voluntary.

Training can be provided at your local community college or online through platforms like **Career Step**.

Once completed, you can take the "Registered Healthcare Documentation Specialist (RHDS)" exam and get certified.

Pay is by work completed, so as your speed improves, so do your earnings. The following companies hire home-based medical transcriptionists:

Athreon
MModal
Nuance
FastChart
Eight Crossings
MT Helping Hand
Inscribe

REMOTE JOB BOARDS

FlexJobs
Indeed
Glassdoor
VirtualVocations
WeWorkRemotely
PowerToFly
JobsPresso
WorkingNomads
Remotive
AngelList
RemoteOk *(mostly tech)*

Companies that let you work remotely

Work from Home Blogs *(some with Job Boards)*

The Penny Hoarder
RatRace Rebellion
WellKeptWallet
RealWaysToEarnMoneyOnline
TheWorkAtHomeWife
TheWorkAtHomeWoman

Final Words

You made it!

All the way to the end - congrats on that!!

I hope you got a lot of ideas and inspiration to add some extra income now as well as build a long term business that you enjoy and that will sustain you well.

As always, feel free to join us in the SassyZenGirl Facebook Group for networking, ongoing support, feedback, partnerships and much more. It's all much easier when you don't have to go it alone:

Join the friendliest Biz Group on Facebook:

SassyZenGirl.Group

If you enjoyed the book, it would be awesome if you could *leave a quick review on Amazon.*

Feedback is always helpful and appreciated and will also help other readers to find the book.

If you haven't already, don't forget to download your free copy of the Cheatsheet:

SassyZenGirl.com/Rookie-Mistakes

And your free copy of the Top Selling Publishing Guide:

BestsellerPublishing.net

That's it for now...:)

I wish you all the very best and much success!! Please share in the group how things have worked out for you - we'll see you over there.

Until then...

Warm regards,

Gundi Gabrielle
SassyZenGirl.com

More SassyZenGirl Yummies

COURSES

SassyZenGirl's Blogging Bootcamp
SassyBlogBootcamp.com

FREE Masterclass:
100K BESTSELLER BLUEPRINT
go to:
100KBestseller.com

Awar∂ Winning
INFLUENCER FAST TRACK
Serie∂

#1 Bestselling
BEGINNER INTERNET MARKETING
Series
"The Sassy Way... when you have NO CLUE!"

#1 Bestselling
TRAVEL BOOKS

Score FREE Flights, Rental
Cars & Accommodations.
Dramatically reduce Airfares.
Get paid to Travel & START a
DIGITAL NOMAD BIZ
you can run from anywhere
in the world!

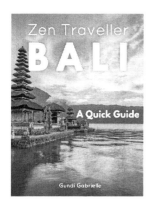

**ZEN TRAVELLER
BALI**
A QUICK GUIDE

Explore the "real" Bali…
The quiet, magical parts
far away from the
tourist crowds…

About the Author

Gundi Gabrielle, aka *SassyZenGirl*, is a Top 100 Business Author and Founder/CEO of SassyZenGirl - #ClaimYourFREEDOM, a platform that helps newbie entrepreneurs turn their passion into a thriving business.

Gundi loves to explain complex matters in an easy to understand, fun way. Her *"The Sassy Way...when you have NO CLUE!!"* series has helped thousands around the world conquer the jungles of internet marketing with humor, simplicity and some sass.

A 12-time #1 Bestselling Author, Entrepreneur and former Carnegie Hall conductor, Gundi employs marketing chops from all walks of life and loves to help her readers achieve their dreams in a practical, fun way. Her students have published multiple #1 Bestsellers outranking the likes of Tim Ferris, John Grisham, Hal Elrod and Liz Gilbert.

When she is not writing books or enjoying a cat on her lap (or both), she is passionate about exploring the world as a Digital Nomad, one awesome adventure at a time.

She has no plans of settling down anytime soon.

SassyZenGirl.com
SassyZenGirl.Group
100KBestseller.com
SassyZenGirl.TV

Instagram.com/SassyZenGirl
Facebook.com/SassyZenGirl

Printed in Poland
by Amazon Fulfillment
Poland Sp. z o.o., Wrocław

29088445R00175